BEST PRACTICE
BENCHMARKING ; 1992

The management guide

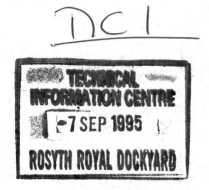
By Sylvia Codling

Industrial Newsletters Ltd, Dunstable, Beds LU5 6BS, UK

First published in Great Britain in 1992 by
Industrial Newsletters Ltd, 42 Market Square, Toddington, Dunstable, Beds LU5 6BS, UK

Desktop publishing by Sally Large

British Library Cataloguing in Publication
Data available on request

ISBN 1 873381 05 0

Manufactured in the United Kingdom

Printed by Jetspeed Printing Services Ltd., 3 Roundwood Lane, Harpenden, Herts. AL5 3BW

First reprint 1993
Second reprint 1994

Contents

Foreword

SYLVIA CODLING has created a unique reference with a truly European perspective. In fact, the many European examples set this Management Guide apart from any others. It is a much needed addition to the existing literature on benchmarking which up till now has been almost exclusively US oriented.

Emphasis is also given to different perspectives with the liberal use of charts and diagrams. Previous thinking on the subject is extended, particularly through inclusion of the softer, behavioural aspects of benchmarking and change management together with the introduction of the supply chain considerations.

The Management Guide also shows the combination of benchmarking and Total Quality Managment (TQM) which is a point that needs to be stressed since benchmarking is a quality tool: the one that sources 'best practices' to feed the continuous improvement efforts of TQM. The case studies, based on European examples, will also be of interest to the reader.

There is more than adequate new material to make this a much needed addition to the art and science of benchmarking. I always welcome new perspectives on this subject and I warmly commend this Management Guide to the reader.

Robert C Camp
Manager, Benchmarking Competency
Xerox Corporation
Rochester NY, USA

July 1992

Introduction

IN TIMES of rapid economic and technical change, profitability and growth come from a clear understanding of how a business is performing, not just against its own results last year but against the best it can measure.

In 1960 the *Harvard Business Review* published Theodore Levitt's landmark paper *Marketing Myopia*. In this, Levitt delivered his research findings which showed that major innovations in any sector come from outside the industry. Yet many firms have continued to look internally or within their industry for clues to achieve or maintain competitive edge. In ever more sophisticated and demanding markets, the need to develop an external perspective has never been more crucial. In today's dynamic environment, benchmarking is potentially the most powerful tool in the strategic armoury.

In North America the technique is a requirement of assessment for the Malcolm Baldrige Award. In Europe it is written into the criteria for the European Company Quality Award. Practical evidence of its power is provided by those who have implemented benchmarking.

Across industry there are examples of how benchmarking has improved performance. For example, it has helped Cummins Engine Company reduce delivery time from eight months to eight weeks; Lucas has reduced the number of shopfloor grades at one of its sites from 17 to four; British Rail has cut cleaning time for a 660-seat train to just eight minutes; and it has helped one company go from the back of the pack in its multi-national group to winner of the coveted Deming Award in Japan. Elsewhere order processing time has been reduced from weeks to just a few days, engineering drawings per man-year have doubled and inventory has been cut by two-thirds.

In 1990, Oak Business Developers carried out its survey into benchmarking awareness and practice in the UK. The overwhelming majority of managers cited lack of knowledge of the concept as the chief barrier to implementation. Since then, interest has mushroomed; so too have conferences, seminars and anecdotal tales of achievement. Even so, now as then, the most frequently asked questions are 'What is it?' and 'How do we do it?'

The objective in writing this book is to answer these questions. It can be read quickly to provide an overview of the subject, its origins and fit within modern management. Through two chapters of snapshots and case histories, plus numerous references throughout the text, it shares the experience and knowledge gained by other benchmarking companies. Last, but by no means least, a substantial portion of the text provides a step-by-step guide to the process, (with planning worksheets provided in Appendix A), for managers who want to get on and do it for themselves.

However, a management tool should never become blunted by bureaucratic constraints and structures. Rather like the Ten Commandments, the 12-step process explained here in detail should be approached as a guiding methodology. All the steps, and their sequence, need to be fully understood to establish direction and context. Understand and learn the process, then teach, train and develop your people so that it becomes second nature to them.

Once understood, however, benchmarking can be adapted to suit the style of both managers and organisation. AT&T has a 12-step process but Xerox Corporation has 10, Royal Mail has eight, Aluminum Company of America (Alcoa) has six, and TNT has five. This does not mean that these companies throw out some steps. It simply means that in practice some steps naturally combine.

Benchmarking is a flexible discipline which has become a way of life in some of the world's leading organisations. Over the past decade, competitive analysis has helped companies understand and improve their relative position. Benchmarking takes over where this ends. From parity to superiority, learning from the best can help your company become the world leader in those factors which are imperative to its success. In so doing, you will gain an enduring and continuously improving competitive edge.

"The pace of events is moving so fast that unless we can find some way to keep our sights on tomorrow we cannot expect to be in touch with today."

(Dean Rusk, *Time Magazine*, 6 Dec 1963)

"You don't have to do these things. Survival is not compulsory."

(W Edwards Deming, *Out of the Crisis*, 1982)

Background to benchmarking

RECORDS dating back to the ancient Egyptians point to the use of benchmarks in construction work. The Egyptians cut a notch in a lump of stone at an accurately determined point, while a flat strip of iron would then be placed horizontally in the incision to act as the support (bench) for a levelling-staff. Using this as the reference (mark) further heights and distances could be measured. The tools have developed as technology has changed, but the word 'benchmark' retains the same meaning in surveying and construction.

For managers and organisations, the word has long been used to denote an acceptable standard, specification or performance. Benchmark setting then evolved as the technique whereby benchmarks (most frequently pertaining to a particular industry or sector) were identified so that companies could devise strategies to ensure they achieved that standard. Thus companies would set a 'hurdle' rate of, say, the rate of inflation plus X% as the minimum acceptable return when judging capital investment proposals.

Major exponents of this technique in the UK are Profit Impact of Market Strategy (PIMS) and The Centre for Interfirm Comparison (CIFC). Since the 1950s PIMS has built up a considerable database of facts, figures, cost and investment ratios for companies in Europe and North America. Using specialised models PIMS can analyse a company's past and present performance. This can be compared with a spread of 'look-alike' businesses in similar positions experiencing similar market growth, fluctuations and circumstances.

Such analyses produce a picture of how a particular business compares with its peers and, more importantly, to what extent it deviates from the 'benchmarks' across a number of operations and parameters, such as purchasing, marketing, research and development, administration, net income, return on investment, and so on. This comparison provides information showing how the company stands in terms of performance, and identifies areas where it is weak or strong when compared with similar businesses. This technique highlights specific areas where significant improvements would have most benefit to overall performance.

CIFC, on the other hand, adopts a similar process to determine management ratios; these show how firms compare with their competitors. The technique, however, while pin-pointing parameters does not show *how* to improve performance.

It should be borne in mind that an analysis which looks only at the results may lead to fallible conclusions. For example, if the analysis shows the firm to be on a par with others in similar circumstances it would lead to complacency. After all, if the target is to perform only in line with the industry standard, there is little to gain from investing to be superior.

Equally, analysis may indicate a firm's performance to be measurably below its peers in several key aspects. An investment decision to improve these areas, based only on this , may not be the wisest course of action. Take for example sales per employee. If this is well below the industry standard the cause may be outdated plant and equipment, overmanning, attitudes, employee morale, and many other factors. Substantial investment in new plant will not necessarily improve the ratio. Obviously, further investigation, particularly of the intangible aspects, would be needed to uncover the real causes. Analysis of the results is not particularly helpful in such instances.

The development of the computer industry throughout the 1960s and 1970s brought a further development in the use of benchmarking.

Multiple suppliers and diverse system configurations made computer selection increasingly complex, particularly for end users that were not always technically sophisticated. Complexities of the buying decision multiplied with the advent of an increasing supply base of personal computers, portables, laptops and mainframes as well as the accompanying array of software. Constantly evolving and improving, the technology facilitated ever increasing configurations to further confuse the buyer. A number of techniques were developed to measure and compare performance. According to an article in the *MIS Quarterly* (March 1985) Byron C Lewis (Department of Decision Sciences, Georgia State University, Atlanta, USA) and Albert E Crews (Data General Corporation, Alabama, USA) stated that of the five most commonly accepted measures only benchmarking had received consistent use as a performance evaluation tool.

Hardware and software suppliers now provide benchmark data in their systems information packages. Performance benchmarks aim to give an 'approximate idea of the kind of performance' the buyer can expect from his/her application.

In the late 1970s benchmarking was pioneered in the realms of management practice by the Xerox Corporation in the US. At that time Xerox was losing a significant share of the lucrative photocopier market to its Japanese counterparts. Investigations showed that the Japanese could sell a unit in the US cheaper than the Americans could manufacture it! Xerox carried out exhaustive analyses of unit production costs in its manufacturing operations and compared these with Japanese counterparts. The company was fortunate in being able to enlist the assistance of Fuji Xerox, its Japanese affiliate, in this work.

Xerox discovered that production costs in the US were much higher than in Japan. The US manufacturing operatives adopted the lower Japanese costs as targets for deriving their own business plans and initiated a benchmarking process to effect the required improvements. This work resulted not only in halting the erosion of Xerox's market share but eventually helped the firm claw back the lost percentage from the Japanese!

In the world of benchmarking, Xerox's use of, and success with, the technique is now legend. It is acclaimed as one of the major factors in the company's revitalisation from its declining position in the 1970s to success in the 1980s. This culminated in the company becoming a Baldrige Award winner in 1991.

Evidence such as this has led to remarkable growth in managements' use of benchmarking in the US throughout the 1980s. The technique has now been incorporated into the Application Guidelines for the Baldrige Award with companies having to describe their approach to selection of world class benchmarks in support of strategic quality planning. Not surprisingly, companies such as AT&T, Du Pont, General Electric (GE), General Motors (GM), Milliken and Motorola all regularly apply benchmarking techniques to critical areas of their operations. Benchmarking networks have sprung up across the US specifically to share the experience and knowledge gained. AT&T undertakes regular benchmarking investigation tours across all industry sectors, willingly passing on the information and experience so achieved through reports and training courses which are also open to other companies.

The benchmarking approach to target setting is steadily gaining a toehold in Europe. Certain industry sectors, insurance for example, are familiar with benchmark setting to establish their target ratios. Companies in these sectors are moving gradually towards a continuous process of comparing themselves against their peers. Leading edge companies, especially those with connections in North America, such as Digital Equipment Corporation, Milliken Industrials (UK) and Rank Xerox, are now developing benchmarking as an integral part of corporate strategy. They are rapidly being joined by those with European parent organisations such as British Steel, British Telecom, ICL, and Shell.

In much the same way as the development of benchmarking in the US followed on that of Total Quality Management (TQM) so benchmarking is achieving a higher profile in Europe through a number of continuous improvement initiatives.

A primary objective of the British Quality Association (BQA) is the promotion of best practice in quality management throughout UK industry and commerce. In this context it has come to recognise benchmarking as an important tool. To enable its members to assist one another in the effective use of benchmarking the BQA organised its first seminar on the subject in March 1991. This was followed rapidly by the creation of a benchmarking committee. The purpose of this group is to promote the spread of benchmarking through seminars, workshops, conferences and regular communication of initiatives and experience.

The UK Government (through the Department of Trade and Industry Enterprise Initiative) recognises benchmarking as an important topic within the larger subject of Performance Measurement. Under its *Managing into the 90s* programme it outlines a philosophy of striving for competitive advantage through Total Quality Management. It sees benchmarking as one of the total quality tools. In early 1992 it published a reprint of its 1989 booklet entitled *Best Practice Benchmarking* which includes eight brief outlines of benchmarking in major UK organisations.

The European Foundation for Quality Management (EFQM) launched the European Quality Company Award in 1991. The application and assessment criteria specify the need for benchmarking to be highlighted in phrases such as how a company measures its performance against that of 'best in class' organisations. The Award, to be made for the first time in October 1992, ensures that companies will require more than a passing awareness of how they compare with the 'best' in key performance parameters. The Award should encourage the spread of benchmarking as occurred with the Baldrige Award in the US.

In Japan, the concept of Kaizen, or Total Continuous Improvement, combined with Dantotsu - striving to be the best - has driven companies to pole position in many industry sectors. Firms realise that their position is vulnerable if they do not continually seek improved ways of operating, irrespective of industry or application. As many companies have learned to their cost, the threat from the East will not diminish. Nor does the threat come only from Japan but also from the rising Tiger

Nations. Some leading companies are turning to joint ventures with former arch rivals to counter the threat - and are themselves posing a threat to indigenous companies. For example, JCB's association with Sumitomo, or Rover Group's involvement with Honda. Others are conducting international benchmarking interchanges across industry boundaries; for example, Cummins Engine Company and Komatsu Limited.

The spread of benchmarking throughout manufacturing, commerce and services is accelerating. In 1989, when Robert Camp published the Xerox experience in his book *Benchmarking: The Search for Industry Best Practices that lead to Superior Performance* the technique was virtually unknown in Europe. In 1990 the first survey into the use of benchmarking in UK companies was conducted by Oak Business Developers. This uncovered certain sectors where it was relatively well-known (insurance, North American off-shoots and so on). Mostly, however, the feeling which prevailed was one of lack of awareness or ignorance of how best to start.

In 1991 the BQA held the first Benchmarking Seminar and by the end of that year two major groups had organised conferences on the subject in London. At the time of writing (1992) there have been three further conferences organised in the UK, plus several in Europe and at least two study tours have been set up to Japan and the US.

Hence, whilst in a sense the seeds of benchmarking have always been around, the combination of climate, experience and necessity now seems set to ensure its rapid growth and development.

Chapter One

What is benchmarking?

Measuring and improving performance

Essential for continuous improvement

An integral part of quality management

BENCHMARKING has been variously defined by dictionaries and companies. Xerox Corporation, which is the pioneer of the technique's application in management practice, defines it as: 'The search for industry best practices which lead to superior performance'. The key words are 'best practice' and 'superior performance'.

Traditional competitive analyses focus on performance parameters, strategies and products within a given industry sector. Such analyses result in a picture of how a business compares with its peers and how much it deviates from the standards, or benchmarks, across any number of operations and parameters. From this a business derives an indication of its relative standing and its comparative strengths and weaknesses. These enable it to set targets to achieve parity with the recognised industry leaders.

Whilst such analyses have a place in corporate strategy they have the potential to inhibit performance improvement and growth. Comparisons with look-alike businesses in similar markets and situations are unlikely to identify or lead to significant breakthroughs which could overturn the paradigms of the sector.

Instead, benchmarking is:

☐ 'An *ongoing process* of measuring and improving products, services and practices against the *best* that can be identified worldwide.'

There are no limitations on the search; the more creative the thinking the greater the potential reward. Unlike competitive analyses, which focus on outputs, benchmarking is applied to key operational processes within a business. It means determining the critical success factors across the organisation. Processes governing those factors are analysed. The best organisations in the world at those processes are established. These are then used to target improvements. Only a thorough understanding of in-house processes makes it possible to recognise and integrate the differences or innovations which will be found in the 'best practice' companies under study.

This understanding comes from adopting a structured, rational approach which benchmarking provides.

Essentially, there are four stages:

☐ Planning;

☐ Analysis;

☐ Action;

☐ Review.

Whilst each stage is important and must be completed thoroughly, the more time spent at the planning stage the less is likely to be wasted later on. 'Review' is a necessary and distinct stage in its own right which also interweaves through the planning, analysis and action phases.

There is another fundamental difference between benchmarking and traditional competitive analysis. Whereas the latter has a suggestion of 'cloak-and-dagger' in its methods of data gathering, often employing industrial 'spies', benchmarking depends for its success on co-operation between partners.

Three types of benchmarking

This need to look for co-operative partnerships has led to the evolution of three distinct 'types' or 'perspectives' on benchmarking:

- ☐ Internal;
- ☐ External;
- ☐ Best practice.

Internal benchmarking

This refers to partners within your company, or division, who may be based at the same, or a different location. So, for example, if you have identified processes dealing with customer complaint handling you could compare practice across different sales departments if they exist on the same site or those at a number of geographically dispersed offices or locations.

Many companies, when they begin benchmarking, start by looking for internal comparisons. There are some good reasons for this, not the least of which is that data are collected relatively easily. Also, the culture and language are the same, surroundings are familiar, communication channels exist, management know each other, and so on.

Internal benchmarking can be seen as the 'nursery' for developing the approach. Processes can be analysed, questions asked and mistakes made in a relatively unthreatening environment. It can provide therefore a sound learning base for the technique. Although internal comparisons are unlikely to result in major breakthroughs they will probably result in 'adequate' returns. Moreover, the results can be effected relatively quickly. If enthusiasm and commitment to the approach are less than overwhelming in the organisation, early small gains from internal benchmarking may provide a necessary injection of energy into the system. In many cases, significant savings do result from the process analysis involved.

One of the side effects of increased globalisation is the move towards harmonisation on best practice, methods or systems existing across a company's world operations. This has happened, for example, at Johnson Group Cleaners (which has 25% of the British market and 2% of the massive North American market - including the biggest US chain).

'The first thing we do (when acquiring a business) is standardise accounting systems immediately,' said the chairman recently. 'The sharing of information between our companies tends to bring out a system of best practice quite naturally.'

Unilever has adopted the approach to monitor and compare costs across its subsidiaries. Whilst highlighting areas of greater cost efficiency it is also challenging long-established habits and practices, leading to even greater cost reductions as processes are refined. For example, fish fingers, which are available currently in seven sizes, in future will be made in only two sizes while the number of margarine tub sizes will be reduced from 19 to nine.

Traditional monitoring systems tend not to highlight duplications and anomalies. A budget exercise which seeks a regular and constant improvement in return rarely demands that managers examine the processes involved. Quite often things 'happen' simply through local custom and habit built up over a number of years. Under the old style management perhaps there was no reason for a manager in one country to ask how something was done at one of the locations of the business in another country. The process focus inherent in benchmarking forces managers to identify each step and, by comparison, learn precisely where savings can be made.

External benchmarking

Many companies progress from internal to external benchmarking. External partners may be found within your own group (in a multinational corporation) but in a different business division. However, they may come from completely different companies within different industries. The fact that the products differ is a benefit rather than a disadvantage since the problems which surround competitive benchmarking can be largely avoided.

The advantage of benchmarking, which looks at processes rather than outputs, is that many diverse businesses share a certain number of general major league processes (those which are essential to run the business) such as warehousing, distribution, manufacturing, and an even greater number of minor league processes (the myriad supports) such as telephone answering, paper handling, accident recording, customer service and so on.

Going beyond discrete product evaluations, benchmarking does more than quantify performance gaps. Although hard processes are compared, an essential part of the approach is the necessity to analyse the management skills and attitudes which combine to make the systems operate effectively. This hidden narrative is as important during the benchmarking exercise as are the visible factors. Often it is a combination of similar processes/different attitudes which determines 'best' practice and may lead to new ways of operating, better use of resources and even process innovations.

The more externally focused the benchmarking exercise the greater the potential for removing blinkers, overturning paradigms and overcoming the 'not-invented-here' syndrome. All too often progress is hampered by the misplaced belief that something 'won't work in this industry because ...'. The 'because' is frequently 'we don't' or 'can't do things that way because we're different'. It is an unfortunate conceit of human beings that they tend to believe, for whatever reason, that 'we know better'. Benchmarking teaches that no single person or company has a monopoly on all the good ideas. It is always possible to learn from someone else.

Recently, much emphasis has been placed, particularly in management articles, on the competitive advantage to be gained from benchmarking. However, the disadvantages of trying to work with direct competitors by far outweigh the advantages.

The most obvious reason is that competitors are unlikely to enter a dialogue with each other, particularly concerning products or processes that are directly competitive. Other problems, such as legal constraints and ethical considerations (perceived collusion for example) also make such dialogue difficult. Also there is the question of whether a competitor can be trusted not to feed misinformation!

Nonetheless, there may be occasions when it is necessary or desirable to consider benchmarking with a competitor. The objective still remains to build a co-operative, on-going relationship. With this in mind, the first step, given an agreement in principle, is to set down a clear legal framework within which it is agreed to work. The information which *is* to be shared, and that which is *not* available, should be defined clearly, leaving no room for ambiguity or future misunderstanding. Once such an agreement is in place, the benchmarking exercise can begin.

There are instances when competitive benchmarking can be highly beneficial. This may apply, for example, where the process in question is one which is particularly critical to an industry. A good example is health and safety in the chemical industry. Du Pont is recognised as the 'best' in this area and has no problem sharing information with other companies, whether in the chemical sector or not. In reality, it is a positive benefit that can ensure the operations in their industry continue to be acceptable to an increasingly environment conscious society.

In summary: external benchmarking is conducted between:

☐ Partners in different industries but the same group of companies, as in the case of large multinationals;

☐ Partners in different industry sectors but sharing similar processes.

Direct competitors should only benchmark with each other in very specific circumstances, where a process is unique to the industry, for example, or where very clearly defined guidelines are agreed on from the outset.

Best practice benchmarking

Benchmarking against best practice requires seeking out the undisputed leader in the process that is critical to business success - regardless of sector or location. The problem is not just to find the 'best' but to define what this means in terms of the process being examined. There are many different perceptions of 'best' according to what is being considered.

Imagine, for example, you are trying to decide which is the best car to buy. You would probably consider what it was most frequently to be used for - shopping or to provide rapid transport from home to office; whether a family car with ample room for children and pets or mainly a one-person transport; how important are factors like safety and fuel consumption and so on. Having defined what influences the decision you can then draw up a short list of models to look at closely. You are then unlikely to waste time looking at a Ferrari if what you need is a small, economical, easily parked car to do the household shopping.

Similarly in business. In the case of best 'telephone response to customers' it could be that the 'fastest' response, or the 'most polite' or 'most helpful' could be defined as the best. The more complex the subject area, the greater attention that must be given to defining the terminology to ensure that Rolls-Royce cars will not be measured against Fiat Unos.

Subsequent chapters of this management guide consider in more detail the importance of defining accurately each word that is used to describe the process under examination, so that each individual fully understands.

At this stage it is sufficient to appreciate that there is no single 'best' practice company. Nor may the partner for one company necessarily be the 'best' for another. A single company may be the 'best' practice partner for a number of others for the same or a variety of processes. The combinations are numerous.

For this reason, the 'best' company to benchmark against will not be found merely by asking a person in another company that is benchmarking its processes. That company is unlikely to have precisely the same considerations. There are no easy answers. The only way to discover which company is 'best' for your organisation is to go through planning and data collection systematically and thoroughly.

Because the definition of what process or which company is complicated and it may take a long time to gather the data, few companies begin their benchmarking experience at this point. Generally speaking, companies will 'practice' with internal partners, progress to 'external' better practice partners and only gradually over a period of time build up to benchmarking against the 'best'.

In the early stages of best practice benchmarking it is important to find a partner that is measurably better in the process which needs to be improved. Once the partner's performance has been matched and (since the aim is superiority not parity) exceeded, the exercise may be repeated as the search for a still 'better' partner or partners continues. Each exercise must be seen as a progression of steps leading to the ultimate 'best'. There is no short cut.

To quote T S Elliott: "Our ends do not know our beginnings". If it is believed from the outset that the 'best' partner will be the first partner, then immediately this could be the first mistake.

Perseverance and practice lead to the 'best'. The motivator is that, of the three approaches described above, best practice benchmarking provides the opportunity to make the most significant improvement, the highest increase on returns and the greatest potential for major breakthroughs.

Chapter Two

Why companies need benchmarking

Striving for superiority

Impact of external conditions

Gives focus to processes

IF THEY are to be effective, business tools and techniques must be suited to the climate and culture in which companies are operating.

Benchmarking provides organisations with a focus on the external environment and an emphasis on increasing process efficiency. In the present climate of dynamic change and fiercely competitive markets both of these are essential for survival.

Fig 2.1 The evolution of technical change

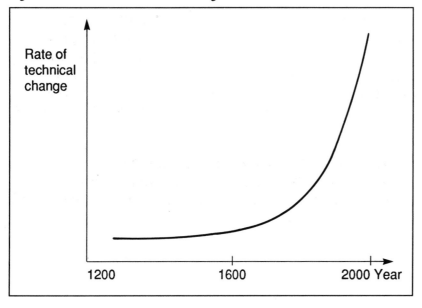

Change is not new; ability to handle change effectively has always been a feature of management. The difference lies in the pace. In the field of technology, for example, where progress feeds on itself to fuel further advances, rapid movement is perhaps to be expected. However, technology has to be directed and driven to meet customer needs. For example, increasing the power of passenger cars requires improved levels of safety, including shorter stopping distances. This in turn has led to the development of anti-lock brakes.

There are more technologists and scientists working in the world today than during the sum total of human endeavour! Products are changing ever more rapidly, even if their function remains the same. Consider the development of the television since the 1950s.

Fig 2.2 Changes in television technology

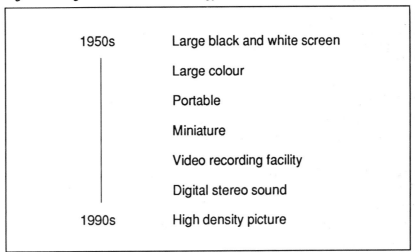

1950s	Large black and white screen
	Large colour
	Portable
	Miniature
	Video recording facility
	Digital stereo sound
1990s	High density picture

However, change is due not only to technological developments but also to political and demographic factors. It is imperative that businessmen keep their fingers on the pulse in order to gauge the effects of change on their operations and planning. This is not unique to the present time; what provides the difference is:

☐ The speed at which change in one part of the world affects another part, due largely to advances in communications technology (eg facsimile machines)

☐ Information technology has made a plethora of data available to organisations, pressure groups and Government bodies. Factors which a few years ago were of little or no relevance, today impinge on companies and have a major impact on how they operate.

Examples of this can be found in the dramatic political shifts resulting from the breakdown of communism (in the former USSR and East Germany), socialism (in Sweden) and apartheid (in South Africa). Mass communications enable political shifts in one country to impact almost immediately on activities in another. The Russian revolution of 1917 may have had little impact on life in America. But a return to 'democracy' in the former USSR in the 1990s has undermined the rationale for mass spending on defence across the world. Two factors, the increase in America's unemployment figures and the restructuring of the British Armed Forces are arguably attributable to this, at least in some measure.

Another example lies in the demographic and social trends that create new demands and generate significant opportunities. A generation has grown up without the wastage of war. Women join the employment pool and stay there with only brief absences for pregnancy and childbirth. More people of employable age are chasing work, whilst technology is removing many of the old manual jobs and replacing them with a demand for skilled knowledge workers.

Fig 2.3 Demographic trends

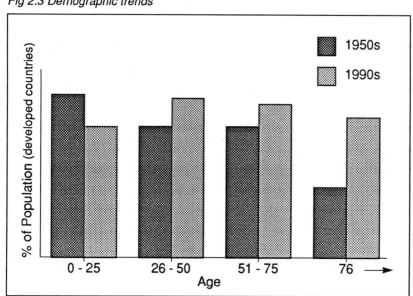

In the western developed nations and Japan there are more elderly people, thanks to the development of health services and pharmaceuticals. At the other end of the cycle, children are being born to older parents and stay in school longer.

In percentage terms, fewer people in work will be supporting an increasing proportion of dependants. Social security and pensions provision will become increasingly difficult issues, whilst the cost of education and re-education has serious implications for the organisation of the future.

Changes on the social front include the restyling of the traditional family; an increase in the number of one-parent households or those where the children in the same family unit have different parents; more working single parent families and an increase in the numbers of latch-key children.

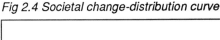

Fig 2.4 Societal change-distribution curve

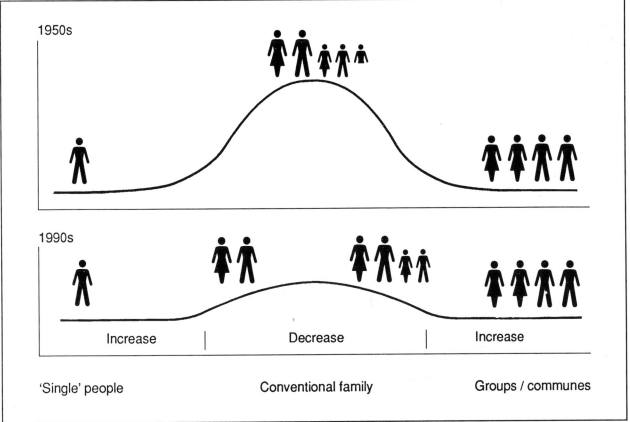

A trend which straddles political and social spheres is the increasing concern for protection of the environment. Whereas this used to be considered a preoccupation of fringe or marginal groups it has rapidly grown to become one of the key issues in strategy and planning.

Added to this, new industries are growing up based on computers, electronics, biotechnology, and information. The business world is bombarded with novel terms - flexible manufacturing, simultaneous engineering, niche markets, just-in-time delivery and manufacturing, total process management, total cost down, electronic data interchange etc etc.

These changes, shifts and trends must be taken into consideration by managers because they directly affect the needs, desires and perceptions of the consumers on whom the organisation depends for its existence. Strategies must, therefore, be formulated in the context of the inter-relationship between the organisation, the consumer and the environment.

Focus on the external environment

This interdependence is a relatively new phenomenon but is increasing in importance. For much of the twentieth century businesses grew without having to concern themselves too much with the outside world. Obviously, they had to take government policies and the economy of the day into consideration when formulating plans but other than that, strategy was based on mainly internal, production-led, factors.

A major shift in attitude came about during the 1960s. A generation of young people grew up with buying decisions based not solely on the fact that something was available. They wanted choice, variety, novelty, colour and innovation. As marketing developed into an essential business function, the department took on the role of the chief link between the company and the outside world. Through activities such as market research, public relations and advertising it was responsible for dialogue with consumers, as well as the image which the company wanted to project. Business plans, however, were still production led. The organisation's activities continued to be governed by internal issues, concerns and objectives.

Fig 2.5 Dinosaurs could not avoid extinction

The traditional budgetary process is a clear example of the emphasis on looking inwards rather than outwards. Targets for the coming year based on past performance plus, say 5%, or on some industry average, are still common even today. Such arbitrary figures bear little relation to external factors and, in a period of rapid change, are meaningless.

Why should 'We've always done it this way' be a reason for doing something? In a rapidly changing world this can lead to extinction - see Fig 2.5.

The number and extent of changes today mean that no person or business can afford to be complacent. The blinkers have to be removed and thrown away. The paradigms, or frames of reference, of the past are little guide to behaviour in the future. When a paradigm shift occurs whole markets are affected. Consider the effect on candle makers of the development of gas lighting. Even this was quickly subsumed by electric lighting. Another frequently cited example is development of quartz watches which reduced Swiss dominance of the market overnight and for many years thereafter.

A wide perspective is necessary to take into account developments and opportunities elsewhere which could fundamentally alter the shape and direction of the market.

External focus, which is a prerequisite for benchmarking, coupled with ongoing and structured data gathering, is one way to keep up with the pace of change. Focusing on processes is another.

Giving focus to processes

Many companies devote considerable time and resources to purchasing and stripping other companies' products down to the minutest detail. Then they rebuild them. This is known as reverse engineering. No matter how sophisticated in application, it can show only the components of a product. It provides little information on how parts were put together and scant insight into the equipment used, or order of assembly. It is a useful, but limited, tool.

Studying the process whereby products or materials are produced is more informative. Two pianists, in the Tchaikovsky Competition for example, given the same piano, music, surroundings, stool and audience, will produce two quite different performances. Only one will win. It is not the piece being played but the way (technique and style) it is played which makes the difference. Only another pianist will be able to understand precisely what distinguishes the two.

In benchmarking it is not sufficient to look only at the product. It is necessary to explore the tangible and intangible factors which combine to produce a superior performance and to involve those people most directly concerned in the activity being examined.

Japanese managers, who understand this, spend some 40% of their time studying and refining processes. Elsewhere, those who have been benchmarking for any length of time confirm that significant and early gains result from this analysis.

Finding a better way to conduct a process can provide the psychological motivation for change. It leads to the acceptance that a different paradigm is possible and, indeed, desirable.

In a complex, dynamic, fast-changing environment companies must strive for superiority in their core activities in order to survive. Competitive edge cannot be achieved or maintained by setting goals based on past, or even present, performance. Benchmarking is itself a process, which helps identify, compare with and emulate best practice wherever it occurs.

Benchmarking is essential to every company as part of the process of continuous improvement. And it has the merit that all aspects of business performance can be raised from the first point of contact (the switchboard, perhaps) to final delivery of the product.

BENCHMARKING AND CHANGE

Benchmarking promotes the climate for change:

A   The gap between present and best practice promotes dissatisfaction and desire for change

B   Seeing, understanding and learning from best practice helps to identify what and how to change

and

C   Witnessing best practice provides a realistic achievable picture of the desired future

Chapter Three

When and where benchmarking 'fits'

Total quality management is the goal

Quality improvements identified

Problem solving understood

DURING the first half of the twentieth century, spurred by shortages resulting from wars, the need to manufacture mass quantities of staple goods spawned large industrial units. These required considerable up-front capital investment. Economies of scale and the need to minimise unit costs were governing factors in the way the organisation was designed and operated.

Production was king and the customer, if he was considered at all, was an ignorant nuisance who could be easily manipulated.

"The customer is an object to be manipulated, not a concrete person whose aims the businessman is interested to satisfy." (Erich Fromm - 'Escape from Freedom' 1941.)

The system encouraged hierarchical management and bureaucratic structures, a trend which was reinforced by growing numbers of holding companies and diversified conglomerates.

The birth of marketing in the 1960s heralded a major change in organisation structure and shape. Over the following 20 years recognition of market needs compelled attention to switch from production-led units to customer-driven operations. Consideration turned to manufacturing flexibility, changing fashions and awareness of concepts such as 'small is beautiful' and 'niche markets'. To maintain and grow market share companies had to deliver what the consumer would buy rather than what factories wanted to produce.

Vertical and horizontal integration faded as the need for market responsiveness grew.

During the 1980s another change was taking place. Global markets and increasing customer sophistication switched attention in the organisation from 'markets' to the unique nature of individuals who comprised them. The concept of quality underwent several changes as it became less something to be controlled than an intrinsic personal element in goods and services. This became a deciding factor in maintaining and growing market share.

Appreciation of the perceptual nature of quality underlined the importance of moving as close as possible to the customer. This was accompanied by stripping out unnecessary activities and concentrating on key strengths. Organisations adopted a flatter structure to quicken responsiveness to customer needs.

"Only those who become attached to their customers, figuratively and literally, and who move most aggressively to create new markets ... will survive." (Tom Peters 'Thriving on Chaos' 1987.)

By the end of the 1980s a combination of increasingly sophisticated customers and economic recession in many countries made markets extremely fierce and gaining significant competitive edge became a constant battle.

Any customer of a bureaucratic organisation knows that frustrations are frequently caused by lack of authority or responsibility at the point of contact. Problems or queries have to be passed across a number of desks or departments and are subjected to delays and varying priorities at each stage. Customers wait days or weeks for a piece of paper or a response which actually takes only a matter of minutes to process.

TAXING MATTERS:

VIC TISHERS was a self-employed management training co-ordinator. His tax returns were lodged with the local office by his accountant and every year he looked forward with despair to the interminable wait and frustration which ensued as his affairs were queried, checked and double checked. It puzzled him that the Tax Office was pretty quick off the mark making demands yet took ages to deal with repayments.

On such occasions, telephone conversations with the officer dealing with his file always led him to believe that matters were being resolved 'as quickly as possible'. His perception of 'quickly' was apparently at variance with the officer's.

Finally, when patience was wearing thin, the Tax Payers' Charter dropped through his letterbox. It prompted him to ask his local Tax Inspector if they might conduct a small experiment. After discussions it was agreed that one of the clerks would monitor the progress of 10 repayment requests through the normal channels. Two factors were to be measured: time taken for the paperwork to pass through the system from receipt to signing off, and time, in minutes, that each repayment request was actually being dealt with by clerks or officers.

At the end of the experiment, the times were averaged out. That taken for paperwork to pass through the system was found to be 28 days; actual time spent on dealing with the forms was 30 minutes.

The root causes were identified as delays occasioned through part-time working and the necessity for countersigning assessments, authorisations and cheques. Consequently, paperwork spent most of its life sitting in 'in-trays' waiting to be dealt with.

Armed with this information the Tax Office was able to implement remedies which significantly reduced delays.

This fictitious parable is an amalgamation of apocryphal comments and should not be construed as referring to any single person or place.

In many cases, moving closer to the customer and understanding customer needs involves empowering employees to ask questions, deal with queries and solve problems. The need for speedier response at every stage increases the need for education in problem analysis and solving techniques.

In recent years the concept of quality has broadened to incorporate every aspect of business operations. In other words, Total Quality Management (TQM) is now the goal. The emphasis is on customer delight and speedier response at every stage of the company/customer relationship.

TQM devolves to individuals the responsibility for improving the service they give their customers, whether these are internal (ie within the same department or company) or external ('strangers' to the company). In broad terms, improvements come from asking what is required by those being served then analysing how far activities or products meet these requirements. The check question is: 'Are they fit for purpose?' If there is a discrepancy, appropriate corrections and improvements are sought and implemented.

Simple problems can be solved relatively quickly. Obscure problems, however, often require detailed analysis by cross-functional teams to unravel the intricate web of interconnecting factors, before symptoms can be cleared away and firm foundations for action detected.

Problem solving processes provide a structured, systematic team approach to identify and analyse root causes, breaking each down to small parts to make it more manageable. The process involves identifying, evaluating and implementing solutions. Review is built-in to ensure that the actions implemented have successfully solved the problem,

Often referred to as 'plan-do-check', this discipline and the team approach required in analysis and evaluation are similar to that applied in the benchmarking process.

Fig 3.1 The basic problem solving model

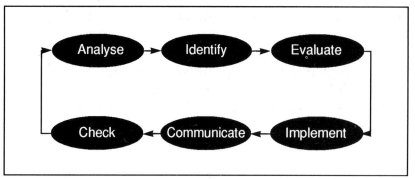

There comes a point, however, when further improvement becomes difficult without reference to the extrinsic environment. TQM ensures that everything is 'fit for purpose' but, other than through customer surveys, provides little feedback from the outside world. An external view of who is doing what, and how, can provide renewed energy, impetus and direction for improvement.

GROUNDS FOR IMPROVEMENT . . .

A COMPANY manufactures boiler tubes at two plants - one in Scotland and another in the US. The person responsible for the cylindrical grinding operation in Scotland heard that his North American counterpart performed the same operation twice as fast. Spurred by this, the Scottish operative used all the quality improvement processes he knew to improve to a speed which was one and a half times that of his American counterpart.

Unable to cut the time further he arranged to visit the US plant. As soon as he walked in to the workshop he spotted the reason for the performance difference. In Scotland only one grinding head was used to run the full length of the tube. In the US two grinding heads were used to run from either end and meet in the middle. The Scotsman returned home, added another head to his machine and managed to produce the parts in less than 75% of the time taken by his American counterpart.

This is where benchmarking dovetails in to the organisation's quality and problem solving activities. Although, in theory, any company can implement it, whether going down the TQM route or not, in practice, the more that quality is ingrained, the easier it is for people to relate to benchmarking. Certainly, it helps if some of the basics are in place. Aspects of Statistical Process Control or BS5750/ISO9000 systems criteria, for example, indicate a readiness to tackle the issues.

Total Quality Management is a long term commitment. It is a powerful force for change and begins to open the windows to the world. However, it has limited ability to monitor developments outside a specific industry sector. Taking some of the tools of quality improvement and problem solving and developing them into the rigorous benchmarking process adds the external dimension which, over time, provides a cutting edge to achieve competitive superiority.

Fig 3.2 The benchmark fit with quality improvement and problem solving

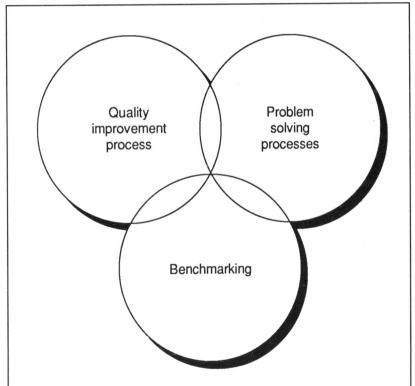

The TQM culture influences the way in which benchmarking develops in the organisation. AT&T, for example, which implemented a successful benchmarking programme, found that teams with a clear view of the organisation's mission and the customer's needs that must be served, are more centred and confident in their activities. With this basic understanding they encounter less of a struggle in focusing their efforts to produce usable results or actionable recommendations. Emphasis on these factors grows as organisations progress along the benchmarking learning curve. In the early stages, it is better to seed confidence in the technique rather than over-control initiatives. Numerous small improvements result from internal benchmarking exercises; the greater their number the more readily confidence in applying the technique will develop.

However, as progress is made and people become more familiar with the application there are greater benefits to be gained from directing energies to the few factors which have greatest significance to the overall performance of the business. This is important before external benchmarking activity begins.

Top level commitment is influential in ensuring that efforts are directed at areas which are of strategic importance to the business rather than those which are 'nice' or 'easy' to deal with. A corporate perspective provides alignment of activities with core values and keeps the ultimate goal in sight. One positive aspect of recession is the focus it gives to critical success factors which organisations have adopted to survive or remain competitive. This is central to best practice benchmarking.

Benchmarking's process focus opens the door into sectors which a business would not normally consider accessible or relevant for comparison. Suddenly it becomes possible to adopt a much broader perspective. Think how different the road network looks to a pilot from 35,000ft up in an aeroplane compared with when he is travelling along in his car. In much the same way, a similar focus in business can identify connections and potential diversions or blocks which could significantly affect a market or industry sector.

After all, even a company that is number one in its industry could see the whole business wiped out by the advent of a technology which makes the sector irrelevant. The conclusion to the boiler tube manufacturer's story (see page 32) makes this point clear.

... **GROUNDED**

The Scottish and American plant operatives mentioned earlier in this chapter continued to vie with and challenge each other to further process improvements. Some while later, despite this, both plants started to lose significant market share. Whilst they had been busy improving against each other, a Japanese competitor developed and transformed the original process to eliminate the need to grind altogether.

Benchmarking first forces analysis of the process to hone it as far as possible, stripping out unnecessary layers, duplications and re-works. Speedier delivery at the requisite quality for the customer is the target. Then it provides the perspective whereby comparison can be made with other companies, industry sectors and geographic locations to identify the significant improvements which can lead to optimum effectiveness.

The result? Delighted customers and superior profit performance in the business's core activities and processes.

Fig 3.3 Impact of benchmarking on TQM

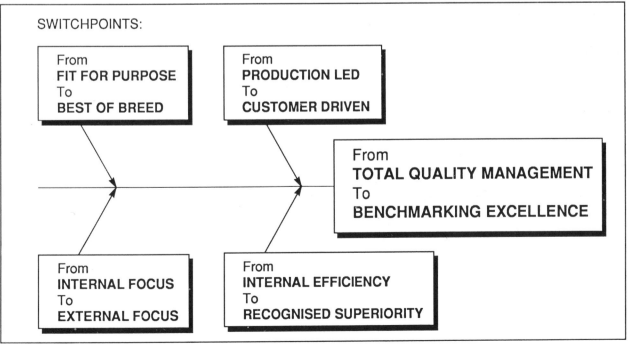

Chapter Four

Snapshots of benchmarking in action

Well established in North America

The 'broken arm' syndrome

The need for networks

THE USE of benchmarking is spreading throughout Europe but most companies which have had programmes in place for any length of time are either based in the US or of North American origin.

Whilst they may not necessarily be the best role models for British or European companies, they have considerable experience of the technique and provide valuable lessons. For this reason, an overview of the world of benchmarking would be incomplete without them.

With any new technique or approach it is difficult at first to gather enough comparable information to begin work. As the number of companies progressing along the learning curve increases, however, this problem is reduced. The 'broken arm' syndrome also applies: if your arm is in plaster it is amazing how many other people you notice also wearing plaster casts! Equally, once a manager broaches the subject of benchmarking it is surprising how many others round the table have something to contribute to the debate.

One of the most effective ways of stimulating the debate is through the development of networks. In the US, where people tend to be more free with sharing information, these have proved an effective way of spreading benchmarking philosophy and experience. Some embryonic groups are being formed in Europe and it is only a matter of time before they too become effective networks.

Those which have started and are growing have provided some valuable lessons in network building. Remembering that the purpose is not to create more work but to work more effectively:

- [ ] Fix a clear purpose for each meeting and elect a chairman in advance;

- [ ] Share the workload by rotating venues between the participating companies' locations;

- [ ] Circulate relevant notes and fix the next date and agenda before everyone leaves the (present) meeting; and

- [ ] Be prepared to give and take in equal measure.

In benchmarking, a piece of information is like an idea; the more it is shared the more it grows.

A number of companies have reported significant benefits from the use of benchmarking. These suggest that positive gains have been made, although the results can take some time to come through.

The examples given here have been accumulated over a period of years from a mix of 'documents in the public domain' and discussions with organisations which have faced these issues. These experiences should inspire many of those standing on the threshold of benchmarking to take the first positive step along this particular path to continuous improvement and ultimate 'best' performance.

1. SIEMENS PLESSEY DEFENCE SYSTEMS

In its early stages, benchmarking is often internal and informal. This may be because the company has not moved far enough down the Total Quality path to be 'ready' for a formal programme. Often called 'harmonisation' of best methods or practice within a company, this can make a worthwhile difference in the way a company operates. The following is one such case.

Siemens Plessey Defence Systems, based at Christchurch in Dorset, is familiar with the reasoning behind benchmarking. However, it considers that a formal process is not possible until the concepts of Total Quality are firmly understood and implemented. Nonetheless, since being take over by Siemens of Germany it has initiated inter-site harmonisation. The purpose of this is to ensure that processes used across the restructured company will emulate the best practice existing at any location within the new group.

2. LUCAS INDUSTRIES

Sometimes the seeds of benchmarking can be seen in other Total Quality initiatives. Consider the case of Lucas Industries.

In 1984 the management at Lucas decided that dramatic action was needed if the company was not to go the way of its Birmingham neighbour, Dunlop. The chairman and his team developed a system called 'Competitiveness Achievement Plans' in which each business manager had to identify the best internal 'rival' anywhere in the world and draw up a plan to close the gap between the Lucas factory and the rival.

In one instance, comparisons were made between the Lucas Heavy Duty Braking Systems plant at Cwmbran and the Lucas Car Braking Systems plant at Koblenz in Germany. Comparing the reward and remuneration systems, for example, led to the number of shopfloor grades at Cwmbran being reduced from 17 to four. In a related exercise, the number of annual pay negotiations has been reduced from five to two.

3. VOLKSWAGEN

Many activities become the subject of benchmarking as a result of an inadvertent comment or casual observation. In such instances, the exercise proceeds without any formal partnership or working arrangement. This was the case some years ago at Volkswagen in Germany which now has a product agreement with Toyota in Japan.

The managing director of a Japanese car company was on a visit to Volkswagen in West Germany. Whilst there he discovered that set-up times on their Schiller 1,000 ton press took two hours. Knowing that the same process, using the same machines, occupied four hours in his own factory he was considerably impressed.

On his return to Japan he challenged his managers to reduce the time to a figure below that of the Volkswagen factory. To help them with this, they enlisted the help of a former chief industrial engineer with Toyota. Six months of hard work followed but by the end of this period the team had managed to reduce the changeover time to 90 minutes.

For a while everyone was happy. Three months later, however, the managing director issued a further challenge: the changeover time should be brought down to just three minutes!

Such a bold goal seemed impossible. The team had achieved what they considered the best possible time already using traditional methods. To meet the new target they were forced to re-analyse and to rethink the entire changeover process and devise a significantly different approach.

Challenging the prevailing paradigms introduced them to a new concept - to externalise much of the changeover work. This meant that the work left to do during machine stoppage time was cut to a minimum. Dies, for example, could be prepared in advance and bolt clamping mechanisms could be simplified; meanwhile tools could be kept close to hand.

Within a further three months the three minute changeover was achieved. Now known as the SMED (Single Minute Exchange of Die) concept, it is an approach which is widely used around the world.

This is a good example of how one senior manager can personally drive the organisation towards superior performance. Recognising that another group is better at a critical process is the first step; challenging their performance is the second and achieving a better result provides the energy and confidence to drive towards a really bold goal.

Had the managing director simply told his managers, when he returned from Germany, that he expected them to cut changeover time from four hours to three minutes they would probably have been thoroughly demoralised. As it was, he let them prove to themselves that they could achieve a better performance than had been possible elsewhere. They then felt inspired to accept the renewed challenge when it came.

4. BRITISH RAIL

The first steps into external benchmarking can be as informal as early internal exercises. 'Keep it simple' is a good way to dip toes into the water and gather experience in the technique.

British Rail's Network South East division conducted a customer survey which showed that cleanliness is second only to punctuality in its customer's priorities. Aware that its record in this area had been unsatisfactory it sought out the best practice.

Eventually this was located at British Airways where it took 11 people just nine minutes to clean through a 250-seat Jumbo Jet. With this target in mind, British Rail developed ways to improve the efficiency of its own cleaning process.

The result: it now takes British Rail cleaners eight minutes to clean up a 12-coach 660-seat train.

5. CUMMINS ENGINE COMPANY

It is more usual that external benchmarking proceeds as a formal partnership where both sides are agreed on the purpose and schematic. The instance at Cummins Engine Company is a good example.

Cummins Engine Company makes marine diesel engines. It used to quote eight months from date of order to delivery. When the recession began to close in Cummins found it was losing business to competitors. It decided to start benchmarking its processes.

One of the most critical areas, in terms of order response times, was found to be assembly on its production lines. Its information gathering processes led it to Komatsu, which produce heavy earth moving equipment. From what it learned, prior to contacting Komatsu, the Cummins team was satisfied that the assembly processes were sufficiently similar to make benchmarking a viable possibility. The team also had evidence that Komatsu's record was significantly better than that of Cummins.

Following the initial contact, when Komatsu agreed in principle to co-operate as a partner, discussion groups were set up and within a relatively short space of time, the benchmarking plan was in place.

A major part of the co-operation involved a five-man team travelling from the UK to Japan. There the team spent several months mapping Komatsu's processes and comparing them with the processes at Cummins. Following its return to England, the team began to initiate some of the modifications it had discovered whilst at Komatsu. Over the next 12 months delivery time was cut from the original eight months to eight weeks. During this time, several other improvements were 'discovered' and these were fed back to the Japanese partner.

Over the next 12-month period, as a result of further modifications to inter-related processes, delivery time was reduced further to eight days. In addition, working capital was reduced to 25% of that in place before benchmarking and the company's market share had been doubled! Furthermore, premium prices could be demanded in some market sectors because of the rapid delivery time compared with the competition.

6. GENERAL ELECTRIC

In most cases benchmarking is introduced to improve the performance of factors which directly affect the bottom line - more efficient warehousing or distribution, for example. However, there are instances where the hidden benefits are at least as keen a motivator. Take, for example, the situation at General Electric (GE).

To counter the tendency towards insularity and parochialism which can be fostered easily in a large organisation, the chief executive officer at General Electric introduced a global best practices programme during the latter half of the 1980s.

This required that managers identified companies across the world which are better at specific aspects of business. They then sought permission to pick the brains of these practitioners. In return, GE promised to share with the better practice companies the knowledge it gained. This effectively amounted to providing free management consultancy services. Direct competitors were deliberately excluded from this programme. When approached by GE to take part, few companies refused and most were flattered to be asked.

In this way, the company approached Ford for ideas on new product development and employee involvement; visited Hewlett Packard for supplier partnership and quality improvement ideas; looked to Digital Equipment for asset management ideas; studied American Express for new ideas on customer satisfaction and investigated Honda for product development initiatives.

An integral part of GE's programme is the site visits made to chosen partner companies. Teams for these generally involve no more than 10 people. Case studies built up through the visits are widely disseminated through the company as well as being included in the curriculum at GE's management development school.

Many advances have been made under this programme but GE adds a cautionary note: The 'best practices' approach cannot address weaknesses until the company is ready to acknowledge that they exist.

Choosing suitable subjects

Commitment and ability to act on findings are prerequisites before any subject is placed under the microscope otherwise the approach backfires and people become demotivated.

The lesson is to not benchmark subjects which are controversial or political. These could include, for example, the number of female graduates retained after a given period, or the number of foreign representatives on the boards of global companies. There is little point gathering information about issues which the company is unable or unwilling to resolve.

The focus should first and foremost be on critical areas of the business' operations. This is not to say that the technique cannot be used to address difficult issues, only that commitment and willingness to change must be present. The more difficult the issue the greater the commitment that is required.

The previous examples show how companies can benefit significantly from co-operating with non-competitive partners. A senior manager at Johnson & Johnson has estimated that this is where 90% of the opportunities for improvement lie, yet 90% of benchmarking companies look only at direct competitors.

There are instances where competitive benchmarking may be beneficial but these tend not to be in areas which lead to significant edge over the competition. Suitable areas include health and safety, for example, where improving against best practice will be to the advantage of the industry as a whole. Du Pont, for example, is a recognised leader in health and safety practice and has become the role model for direct competitors as well as for companies outside its sector. Other subject areas for useful competitive benchmarking are environmental protection, pollution control, community support; in other words, factors which concern industry as a whole.

As a general rule, however, it is advisable to avoid benchmarking against direct competitors. Many companies are imbued with a culture which believes in mistrusting and misleading the competition. How can the team be sure the information it is given is correct?

There is also the disadvantage that comparing practices with another company with closely resembled products may provide a blind to potential trouble-spots or new rivals. The biggest and most sudden threats often come from entrants which are not constrained by the paradigms of the industry. Whilst being intent in trying to improve a process against a competitor, others may well come along with a system which does away with the need for it altogether.

Nonetheless, competitive benchmarking is still pursued by some as the following short examples show.

7. COMPETITIVE BENCHMARKING

In the late 1980s a large North American manufacturer of vehicle engines began to lose market share. It received poor engineering ratings from customers and could not understand why.

It took the decision to benchmark its competitors' engineering departments, asking customers specifically what they liked about the competitors' engineering and what they did not like about the company's approach. They also employed a specialist firm to find out, by directly asking the question: 'How do competitors allocate their engineers?'. This firm knew that the solution lay in casting the net wide: half the sample contacted can usually be relied on to give information. The larger the sample, the more information is gathered. Through this form of benchmarking, the engine manufacturer found that the most successful companies assigned up to 200 of their engineers to work full time at their customers' car factories. By contrast, it allocated only 10 engineers to work directly with customers.

Although the engine manufacturer had been aware that the competition adopted this approach they were not aware of the extent. Nor did it realise how much customers valued this aspect of the service. The engine manufacturer therefore adjusted its resource allocation and, as a result, avoided losing a major contract.

This example shows why competitive benchmarking can be less than satisfactory.

Firstly, there was no direct dialogue between the engine manufacturers. Hence, any opportunity there might have been for capturing nuances of style and attitude, which play a significant role in co-operative benchmarking, was missed.

Secondly, the measure used (allocation of engineers to customers) was a finite one and of limited use. A more meaningful measure might have been number of man hours spent by engineers at customer premises or hours allocated to product development compared with hours for fire-fighting. This might have shown that 30 effective engineers could do the jobs of two or three times the number of less effective ones.

Thirdly, the end result was a one-off improvement against the single measure with no evidence that ongoing improvement could be built in. Yet a benefit of benchmarking is the ongoing opportunities it provides for improvement.

8. COMPETITIVE ANALYSIS

Sometimes the boundary between good competitive analysis and competitive benchmarking can be a little blurred.

A large, well-known hotel group decided to conduct a competitive benchmarking exercise to help it decide whether or not to move into a new market sector. Accordingly, it sent a team of six employees on a six-month information gathering mission round the country to compare hotels in the target sector.

As well as gathering facts such as quality and number of towels per room, variety and quality of shampoos, bath salts, soaps and so on, the team tested out the hotels' response times to guest requests (for example, for more coat hangers, new shoelaces), sound insulation between rooms, general friendliness of service and the willingness of staff to help.

At the end of the six-month period the team submitted their report about potential rivals, their strengths and weaknesses and the perceived opportunities. Armed with this information, the hotel group budgeted for a new chain of hotels which they felt would beat the competition in every respect, from soap to service to soundproof rooms.

A year after launching, this new chain of hotels had an occupancy rate 10% higher than the rest of the industry.

9. GPT

There is no single best route into benchmarking. What sets leading companies apart, however, is the determination with which they apply benchmarking for continuous improvement in order to gain and maintain an edge in fiercely competitive markets. Our final snapshot provides an excellent example of this.

GPT Limited was created in 1988 following the merger of the telecommunications businesses of GEC and Plessey. Although both were leaders in the UK and had strong sales in a number of export markets, a global presence was required to compete effectively in the fast moving telecommunications sector. A major initiative was launched to combine efficiently and effectively the resources of the two companies in order to address this goal and to forge the new corporate culture which it required. The subsequent training programme involved all of GPT's staff and earned the company a National Training Award.

GPT became jointly owned by GEC (60%) and Siemens (40%) following the takeover of Plessey. The combined telecommunications business of GPT and Siemens and their international experience makes them world leaders.

The strategic change process was continued with part of the programme being concentrated on increasing competitive advantage. The two pertinent questions were: how to improve performance and market leadership and how to develop innovative products and services to enter new markets? One of the techniques which created much interest was competitive benchmarking. So much so that the GPT Board decided to launch a specific initiative.

A pilot project covering three major topics was completed in June 1989. The main purpose of this was to investigate the technique and how it could be applied effectively in GPT. One of the learning points was the lack of understanding of problems which existed. It often seemed the deeper one dug, the more elusive the answer became.

However, persistent analysis overcame this hurdle and the results of the pilot were conclusive. Benchmarking was seen as an essential tool for a successful business. Consequently, the GPT Board sponsored a second phase of projects to train and develop capability in the technique. Twelve key topics were selected for benchmarking and a series of seminars was incorporated to facilitate the learning process and share information and contacts.

The second phase was a resounding success! Along the way the company was voted the best overall performer in a major independent business survey of PABX customer satisfaction. However, whilst winning awards is satisfying it is only a way of keeping score. GPT believes that one of the most significant benefits of benchmarking is the acute extenal focus which it develops. The technique is now firmly established to augment the customer focus policy and as an ongoing process in the company's day-to-day activities.

Chapter Five

Overview of the benchmarking process

No hit-and-miss process

Requires and imposes discipline

Demands understanding of the business

As seen in Chapter Three, effective benchmarking is best approached in the spirit of Total Quality Management. The philosophy behind this provides the necessary human elements of empowerment, enthusiasm and cooperation which effect positive change and help gain commitment to continuous improvement.

Benchmarking is not hit and miss. Nor is it a technique which can be picked up and dropped at whim or according to availability of resources, usually time. There will always be people who look for panaceas and instant puddings and who feel this may be it. Equally, there will always be those who believe a little of something is better than nothing at all. Approached in this way it is best left well alone.

Benchmarking is a process. Its overriding characteristic is the discipline it requires and imposes. Rigorously following a logical sequence of steps enables managers to identify what is most important to the business, where improvement is most needed and in which areas, if there is more than one, it would have the most significant impact on performance.

The process encourages, but also demands, intimate understanding of the business before comparisons can be made, gaps identified or actions implemented. The goal, which is always to achieve competitive superiority, can only be realised over the long term.

As with any process, there are Inputs, several of which, as the Fig 5.1 shows, are 'soft' or intangible factors, and others which are 'hard' and quantifiable; as well as Activities and Outputs.

The intangible inputs

It is wise to assess, review or gather the necessary inputs before starting any exercise. In benchmarking the inputs may vary according to the particular process under the microscope but three of the basic requirements are vision, commitment and diligence.

Before any major initiative is undertaken, there must be a vision in place of where the organisation will be as a result of the initiative. Otherwise how will people know where they are going or whether they are heading in the right direction? A popular Chinese phrase adopted by David Kearns, president of Xerox Corporation during the first decade of its benchmarking programme was: 'If we don't change direction we might end up where we're headed.'

The fact that a benchmarking programme is being considered implies a *desire and a need for change*. However, there is always resistance to change and it is normally in direct proportion to the degree of change required. This resistance can be overcome by providing the motivation to live with the uncertainty along the journey. If benchmarking is thought of as the vehicle, then vision is the fuel which keeps it going. However, since it is a never-ending journey, the fuel must be something sustainable and renewable.

Fig 5.1 Benchmarking - the overview

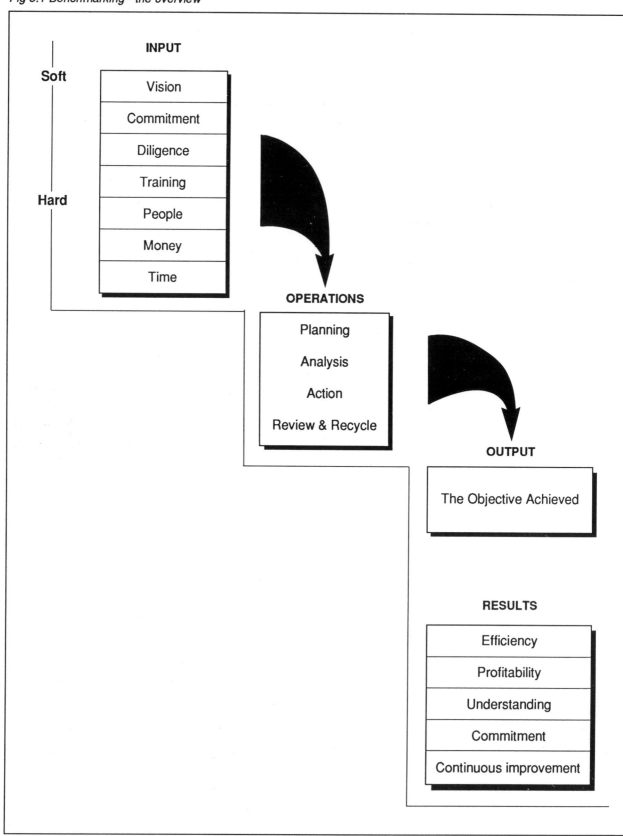

Vision is essential for change

The most effective vision should be:

- ☐ Inspirational, so that people will be prepared to dedicate extraordinary effort when required, and

- ☐ It must be realisable.

In other words, although vision stems from creativity and lateral thinking and so inhabits some nebulous world, it must be brought down to earth and described with enthusiasm and conviction. And it must include some pointers as to how it can be achieved. Utopian visions are fine for personal dreams but do not translate readily into the harsh realities of the business world. Show people the stepping stones and the chances are they will believe they can walk over water.

It also helps to think of benchmarking as *just one of a number of vehicles* in which to make the journey. People are more likely to come on board if, along with a clear vision of where and why they are going, they understand how the preferred vehicle is going to take them there. No matter how inspirational or idyllic a palm-fringed, peaceful island may be, if the only way to arrive is to paddle 6,000 miles through shark infested waters in a canoe with no support or defence devices, not many will want to make the effort!

The vision input to benchmarking is the desire to achieve superior status, expressed as *'becoming the best'*.

Each person's interpretation is different and there is no single 'best'. The field is wide open for every company to be the best at something. Real vision implies knowing what the core 'something' is for your particular company or organisation and how it can be achieved.

There are two facets to vision: corporate vision and the benchmarking team vision.

Corporate vision is the overall vision of where the organisation is heading and how benchmarking will help make arrival easier. Much of the success of the Xerox and General Electric programmes has been attributed to the visions of David Kearns and Jack Welch - the two chief executive officers respectively - and the vitality with which they shared this. The higher the source of the vision the more zealously it is likely to be followed.

The benchmarking team vision, on the other hand, is much different. Any group involved in a change process encounters resistance and occasional hostility. Individuals within such a group need to share a common vision of where their efforts are leading them to give them the inner strength to overcome negativity. It needs to be clearly stated in words that everyone agrees and understands; otherwise, in the real world, how will anyone know if it has been achieved?

Commitment increases the success rate

Benchmarking requires considerable time, investment and effort. The second input therefore is commitment - with a capital 'C'. The greater this is, the better the chance for achieving results.

The ideal combination is a high level of personal commitment from employees throughout the organisation coupled with audible support from as high up the organisation as possible. Commitment from employees can be gained by senior management effectively and enthusiastically communicating the vision and voicing their support for benchmarking to achieve this. Commitment from high up within the hierarchy depends on buy-in by the chief executive officer or chairman and his executive team. Time invested in securing this from the outset will speed progress with the benchmarking programme.

Inevitably there will be occasions when benchmarking leads to a change of policy, or decisions or investments need senior level sanction. The more critical the area being benchmarked, the higher the level of commitment required to secure support in these areas. If senior executives are on board from the outset much time is saved between the planning and action phases of the benchmarking process.

It is normal for there to be a long lead time between the start of the benchmarking exercise and achieving the improvements attributable to it. The commitment, therefore, must be more than just verbal.

There are a number of other ways in which it can be expressed, for example:

☐ The financial support which will be given to the process - a reasonable budget for planning and research, for example;

☐ Other support resources such as time and facilities available for team meetings, activities and communications;

☐ The emotional support that will be made available from internal and external sources, either to act as sounding boards during periods of low morale or 'expert' help with the technicalities of the benchmarking process;

☐ The corporate support which can be shown by featuring benchmarking objectives and success stories in House editorials or displaying information across all sites on notice boards; and

☐ Integrating benchmarking objectives into personal appraisal, remuneration and reward systems.

Diligence makes the transition possible

Benchmarking is a continuous process, with the sequence of steps arranged in logical order. Each requires its own input from the previous one as well as providing the input to the next one. Diligence in following the sequence and in completing each step thoroughly is therefore the third input.

There are several misconceptions about benchmarking. One of these suggests that benchmarking consists of deciding something needs to be improved, making a few visits to perceived 'better' companies and then initiating relevant improvements. The mental time frame which accompanies this thinking is on a scale of days or weeks at most. Such visits have been variously dubbed:

- ☐ 'Industrial Tourism' - in which people go visiting just to see what there is to see because it happens to be there.

- ☐ 'Feel Good Trips' for people who go visiting other companies, just to see that what they do is not as impressive as they had been led to believe and come back feeling good about what they themselves do.

- ☐ 'Wow! Visits' in which the visitor sees companies doing wonderful things and comes away thinking 'Wow! If we did that we could be as good as them'.

The following dialogue is commonly heard:

A: 'We ought to install a new accounting/ordering/ product launch/telephone system. Which firm shall we visit to benchmark against?'

B: 'What is it you are looking for?'

A: 'We don't know. That's why we want to go and look at what other people are doing.'

B: 'What is wrong with the present system?'

A: 'We don't know if there is anything wrong until we see something better.'

B: 'How will you recognise what is better?'

A: 'We won't know until we see it.'

B: 'What exactly does the present system involve?'

A: 'Well, roughly ..... x, y and z.'

In other words, it is taken for granted that the visit will provide all the questions and all the answers! Not so.

Correctly applied, benchmarking can replace 'Wow' with 'How'. Diligence is what makes the transition possible.

It must be applied at every stage of the benchmarking process but is perhaps most critical at the planning stage. There are good reasons for this:'

☐ Even if the team has nothing better to do than waste their time on a potentially abortive or fruitless visit, it owes it to the host company to show respect for theirs.

☐ It does not help the team's reputation to be seen to be undecided about the information it is aiming to gather.

☐ Bear in mind all the time that the people to talk to are also potential customers or PR agents for the company. The team should think of the impression it is creating.

☐ Support for the team's activities is unlikely to be high if it cannot clearly communicate its objectives and goals.

☐ If the team has little understanding of what is happening in its own organisation, how will it know if another firm is better or worse?

Hard inputs are essential also

In addition to the combination of soft inputs there are essential hard inputs, for example people, time, money, physical resource and training.

☐ **People**. The people dimension depends on the degree of vision and commitment shown by the chief executive and the senior management team. If a manager has support from superiors he is more likely to give his or his people's time for benchmarking activities. Similarly, the people will themselves be more dedicated to the process if they are convinced of support and know that their efforts will be rewarded.

☐ **Resources**. The allocation of financial and physical resource will flow from the soft inputs. Diligence plays a significant role in establishing the credibility to secure resources. Accurate planning of activities will ensure that the optimum resources are requested or allocated to gain the desired results.

☐ **Training**. Training is an important element but the best time to feed it in to the process depends on a combination of factors. For example: how high is the general awareness level of benchmarking? Is commitment/awareness/skills training necessary? What is being benchmarked? How many people are involved and when? What order of priority/significance is attached? What level of understanding or skill is required?

Fig 5.2 Benchmarking process operational steps

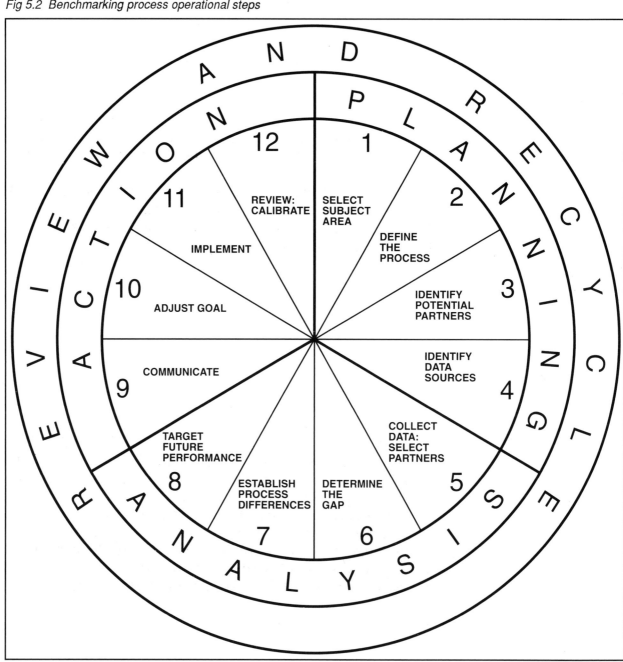

Problems can still arise even when the senior executives are well versed in the technique, convinced of its efficacy and committed to its implementation throughout the organisation. Responsibility may be devolved to business units but with insufficient or no training, little positive benefit may result.

It is advisable to audit the level of awareness, knowledge and skills present and required before launching the programme. If training is needed it should be planned to take place at appropriate stages.

Remember, benchmarking is not meant to create more work, it is intended to produce more effective work. Training helps in achieving this.

Activities in the benchmarking process

Having put the inputs in place, it is now possible to look at the activities of the process. As detailed in the following chapters, there are four distinct operational stages each comprising a sequence of steps.

☐ STAGE 1. Planning

☐ STAGE 2. Analysis

☐ STAGE 3. Action

☐ STAGE 4. Review and recycle

Each stage must be completed as thoroughly as possible before moving on. In practice, the bulk of time is spent at the planning stage. An 80%:20% split between Planning and Analysis is a good average for most benchmarking exercises. Action depends on implementation so the time involved will vary widely from one exercise to the next. Along with Review and recycle, it is ongoing so the measurement of time involved may not be a relevant or accurate guide.

STAGE 1.   Planning

STEP 1. Select the broad subject area in which to benchmark - manufacturing, warehousing, marketing, for example.

STEP 2. Define the process within that subject area which is to be benchmarked - eg changeover time, picking, or a new product launch.

STEP 3. Preliminarily identify the potential partners against which benchmarking may be possible and beneficial.

STEP 4. Identify the most likely sources of data to substantiate initial perceptions and select the most appropriate method of collection.

STAGE 2.   Analysis

STEP 5. Collect the data and from these confirm the most likely benchmark partners which should be contacted.

STEP 6. Determine the gap between the existing performance and that produced by the benchmark company. Contact and arrange to visit the benchmark company to validate or substantiate information.

STEP 7 Compare the existing process with that at the benchmark company and establish the differences, enhancements and modifications.

STEP 8. Target future performance to take into account process improvements.

STAGE 3.   Action

STEP 9. Communicate benchmarking objectives and results throughout the organisation, the outside world and the benchmarking partner where possible and relevant.

STEP 10. Adjust goals in the light of desired performance improvements stimulated by comparison with benchmark partner; and develop corrective improvement plans to achieve these.

STEP 11. Implement and monitor the corrective improvement plans.

STEP 12. Review progress and calibrate performance improvements and targets.

STAGE 4. Review and recycle

Although shown as the fourth stage, this nevertheless has two guises. It is the last of the 12 sequential steps in the process of benchmarking, but it also interweaves at various points throughout the Planning, Analysis and Action stages.

For example, collecting the data and selecting benchmark partners (Step 5) may throw up some information previously not available o help identify potential benchmarking partners (Step 3) which necessitates a Review of the partners previously listed.

Similarly, determining the gap (Step 6) in the light of detailed information from the benchmark partner may not be possible without more work on the in-house process definition, resulting in the need to more exactly define the process (Step 2).

Since it is difficult to know in advance how much reviewing and recycling will be appropriate the main point is to allow contingency time when planning the benchmarking exercise. Without this there is a danger that the team feel pressured to report back by a fixed date with unprofessional or incomplete recommendations.

Outputs can be difficult to measure

'Output' is frequently confused with 'Result'. A quick rule of thumb is that an output is always measurable, (eg weekly production per machine, current delivered by a circuit, or information produced by a computer) or visible (a machine/carton of milk/sheet of steel). A result, on the other hand, may be either quantitative or qualitative (the score of a sporting contest or the consequence of an action).

Translated into benchmarking, the output should reflect the measurable achievement of the objective of the exercise. This may be directly quantifiable in terms of 'cut machine down-time back by 75%'. Alternatively, it may be measurable from indicators, such as 'customer satisfaction increases':

- [ ] Repeat orders up by X%;
- [ ] Order size increased by Y%; and
- [ ] Incomplete orders down by Z%.

Whenever the output is uncertain, or not directly measurable, the short cut is to ask 'which indicators reflect this output?' and then assign measures to those indicators. If indicators cannot readily be identified, then possibly the process is not correctly understood or has not been accurately mapped.

Outputs are considered often to be most difficult to measure in the service sector. Service, however, is always the result of the process which delivers it. Where a process exists, output indicators can always be found and measured.

Results may be difficult to isolate

Benchmarking is an on-going process which eventually melds to become another facet of corporate culture. Although results are difficult to isolate, some which have been cited by practising companies include:

☐ **Greater efficiency**. This is an almost inevitable result of analysing, understanding and 'tidying up' existing processes even without benchmarking. When comparisons are made with similar processes elsewhere, further efficiencies result.

Good benchmarking companies make it a habit to assess and improve the process whilst helping and training people to work to the best of their ability. This ratchets up the efficiency of the operation still further.

☐ **Improved understanding**. Involving people in benchmarking results in improved appreciation across the broad spectrum of a company's activities on a number of different levels.

Firstly, since teams from across the organisation are involved each member gains understanding of operations from different perspectives. The longer that benchmarking continues, the more people learn to respect and understand the importance of other players in the team and the organisation.

Secondly, since it is impossible to benchmark effectively without thorough knowledge of the systems and processes, increased understanding of how and why these interact is gained.

Thirdly, good benchmarking relies on effective corporate goals and missions. This means that corporate leaders are required to think through and communicate these clearly; and employees gain greater insight than might be the case without a benchmarking programme.

☐ **Heightened commitment**. This results from a combination of greater efficiency and understanding plus the engagement of all people in the organisation. Whenever involvement is encouraged, self respect grows and greater commitment results.

As the old Chinese proverb says:

'Tell me, I may hear
Show me, I may remember
Involve me, I will understand.'

☐ **Continuous improvement**. This is the prime justification for benchmarking. Some people worry whether continuous improvement or superiority can be maintained if every company is benchmarking against the best. However, not all managers who see best practice find the means to implement it in their own organisation. Added to which the goal posts are movable. There will always be innovators, technology will always improve and some people will always strive to improve beyond the best that currently exists.

☐ **Increased profitability**. Improving operating efficiency to become more competitive is one of the prime motivators for Total Quality programmes. It is difficult to assess in hard financial terms with complete accuracy how much of an increase stems from a particular initiative. There is, however, consensus among practising companies that benchmarking is an extremely powerful tool. It highlights duplications, disfunctions, anomalies and bad practices enabling these to be removed and replaced by better practice. This results in increased efficiency, lower cost, improved cash flow and better profitability.

Chapter Six

The planning stage: Processes

Master the basics

Systematic approach is necessary

Complete each process step

THERE is no need to invest large sums of money in a top of the range car in order to learn to drive. The ability to accelerate from 0-60mile/h in under 6s is uninspiring when the learner is still trying to master the rudiments of start, go and stop!

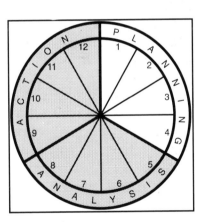

Similarly with implementing benchmarking. It is not necessary to begin with a model exercise that is the envy of everyone and will be watched and monitored with anxious interest. It is better to master the basics in an everyday 'test-bed' or 'trial run' situation which does not arouse too much attention elsewhere in the organisation but could make a sufficiently noticeable improvement to convert some of the inevitable sceptics.

In such situations it may be less important to consider each step in detail than to find out how the overall model works and gain a degree of confidence in the approach. However, once the basics have been mastered, a more systematic sophisticated approach enhances performance across a variety of situations. The more crucial the need for improvement, the more important it becomes to pay rigorous attention to completing each step of the process.

The first four steps making up the planning phase are the most time-intensive of any benchmarking exercise. Experience has proved repeatedly, however, that the quality of result achieved is directly related to the effort invested at the outset. In this chapter we discuss the first two of these which concern the selection of processes.

STEP 1. Selecting the subject area to benchmark

Companies adopting the 'trial runs' approach to benchmarking tend to choose the subject area as the result of another initiative. For example, it may be selected as a result of a problem solving exercise or come to light through a customer survey. Topics with an immediate impact such as delivery scheduling, complaints and telephone handling could fall into this category. Solutions tend to be reactive, the priority being on implementation in the shortest possible time to effect a result. Benchmarking makes a valuable contribution in these situations but such shortfalls may be dealt with by standard problem solving (or similar) mechanisms.

In major benchmarking projects, however, the starting point is identification of a subject area within which improvement is critical. It is a focused approach. It is not a case of throwing a clutch of ideas into a hat, pulling one out and going to work on that, or on one person's pet subject.

The criteria for selecting the subject area are:

- [ ] That it should be of strategic importance to the business; and
- [ ] Improvement in that area will make a significant contribution to overall business results.

It is important at this early stage to paint on a broad canvas. The obvious ideas are not necessarily the best ones. People cannot help becoming involved in their own speciality to the exclusion of wider business concerns. The possibility of tunnel vision should be acknowledged and the opportunity taken to generate a wide variety of ideas. Tools such as brainstorming are effective for this purpose. Outside 'experts' may help if the organisation has difficulty focusing on external as well as internal factors.

Answering the following questions may help with identification and clarification.

[ ] *What business are we in?* This may be obvious but beware of taking it too much at face value.

This question does not generate the answer to 'What to Benchmark?' It is, however, a basic question to address in any strategy formulation exercise. For example, when television became available to a mass market in the 1950s, Hollywood producers, who thought they were in the business of making films, felt threatened. They saw their market decline, as more people stayed in to watch television and fewer went out to see movies. Had they realised they were in the business of popular entertainment rather than making big screen movies they might have co-operated with television producers instead of trying to compete against them. Their market could have grown phenomenally instead of declining.

[ ] *What must we do to remain in business?* This means the core activity(ies) without which the firm could not be in business.

Basic survival factors, such as operating within the law and birthright issues, like paying bills, are not included here. It is assumed these are at least adequate!

☐ *What must we do to be really successful in our business?* These are factors which distinguish leaders from followers.

The answer is not simply 'Make X% profit' or a variation on that theme. It is the activities in which the business has to excel to generate the returns which satisfy the business's success criteria. As such, there may be several answers.

☐ *What single factor would make the most significant improvement to our customer/supplier/employee relationships?*

In answering this question both internal and external customers/suppliers should be considered. The quality of internal relationships has a distinct impact on external ones.

This question should provoke creative thoughts. It is not sufficient to consider the world as it is; imagine what it will be like in, say, five or 10 years and then ask what would significantly improve relationships. The aim is to generate ideas without constraints imposed by current, short-term, economics or politics. The list can be analysed later to identify and prioritise key improvements.

☐ *What areas, if improved, would make the most significant contribution to our bottom line results?* No business can afford to ignore this question but it should be a qualifying, rather than a primary question to address.

If placed higher up the order there is a danger this factor may dominate, causing other answers to be framed only in financial terms. This may overshadow creative thinking and restrict possibilities for improvement.

Brainstorming is one method of generating a number of ideas for possible subject areas. The first two questions above establish the broad canvas while the remainder direct the focus. The following box illustrates a typical question and answer sequence for a videotape manufacturer.

Question 1:	What business are we in?
	Home entertainment
Question 2:	What do we have to do to remain in business?
	Obtain rights to films *Efficiently produce video copies* *Effective marketing* *Fast distribution*
Question 3:	What must we do to be really successful?
	Be the best supplier of most popular videos
Question 4:	What would make the most significant improvement to our customer/ supplier/employee relationships?
	Faster delivery on demand to customers
Question 5:	What area, if improved, would make the most significant contribution to our bottom line?
	Increased market share as a result of more effective distribution

The objective is to establish a maximum of three subject areas in which benchmarking would make a considerable impact. These are then prioritised. It is wise to direct attention to a small number of areas, particularly in the early stages of benchmarking when knowledge of the technique needs to be developed alongside the process itself. It will prove difficult otherwise to prioritise key processes to benchmark.

The question to bear in mind is: *Is this what is **really** important?*

Difficulty in agreeing this could signal too narrow a focus. The strategic overview - imagine taking an aerial photo of the business - should extend from suppliers through employees to end users.

Defining the subject area:

☐   What business are we in?

☐   What must we do to stay in business?

☐   What must we do to be really successful?

☐   What would make the most significant
      improvement to our customer/supplier/employee
      relationships?

☐   What area, if improved, would make the most
      significant contribution to bottom line results?

☐   Is this **really** important?

Worksheets 1 and 2 help focus on subject areas. They
can be found at Appendix A

Supply chain

Selection of the subject area may be influenced by the company's, or function's, position in the supply chain. This is the complete string of events leading up to delivery of the product or service to the end user. Although it is likely to play a less significant role in 'trial runs' than when benchmarking is drawn into the strategic armoury, identification of the supply chain is an important element in gaining an overview.

For example, in many manufacturing companies, costs associated with suppliers account for as much as 50% of the total cost of goods. Additionally, for those components or sub-assemblies which a company does make for itself, more efficient external sources may be available. Identifying and taking advantage of these could increase the number of supplier contacts and, consequently, their influence on cost of goods.

Any company, or function, which depends on suppliers for half or more of the total cost of goods could find that supply management is a more important subject area in which to benchmark than say, production, distribution or customer service. The closer to the beginning of the chain that improvements can be identified the less waste is built-in or carried forward to subsequent stages. The inefficiency-multiplier effect is thus reduced. Superior handling of functional and cross-functional supply management processes may have greater impact on profitability and competitive position than, say, speeding up new product launches or improving sales planning.

Supply management: How efficient is it?

☐ What is the total number of suppliers the company deals with?

☐ Are there secondary or back-up suppliers?

☐ How competitive are the company's suppliers in the world market?

☐ How well are they managed by the company?

☐ How are supplier quality assurance or evaluation managed?

☐ How effective is the management of cross-functional processes that promote good supply management, such as the strategic make v. buy analyses?

The real value of focusing on the supply chain lies in:

☐ Identifying suppliers in the correct sequence;

☐ Considering what are the critical inputs to each stage of the business;

☐ Recognising the extent of their influence on the business.

Drawing a model of the business's supply chain helps clarify thinking. Seeing the overall picture also makes the detail easier to absorb. Not all real-life examples will be as straightforward as the simple model shown here however!

Fig 6.1 Tea supply chain model

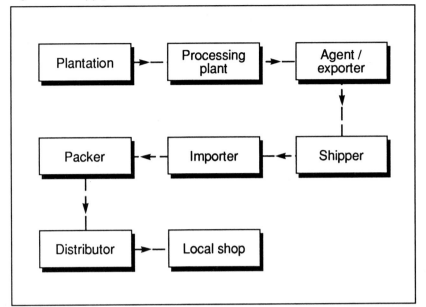

Worksheet 3 for drawing up a supply chain model can be found in Appendix A

STEP 2. Define the process to benchmark

Having identified the subject area in which to focus attention, the next stage is to select the precise process which will be central to the entire exercise.

Process definition is one of the most critical steps in a benchmarking exercise. In fact, since much of benchmarking is comparing processes, it is difficult to complete some of the subsequent steps without spending sufficient time analysing, questioning, rationalising and validating this. There are no 'quick' ways to do this. In any mature organisation, processes will be numerous, complex and linked by an intricate and often tangled web.

As with any complex exercise the best place to start is at the beginning and proceed in a logical fashion!

Visualise a large Spanish onion:

Fig 6.2 Every organisation has layers of processes

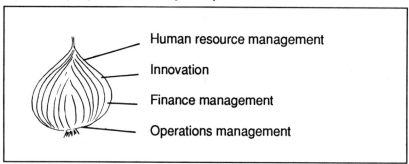

Human resource management

Innovation

Finance management

Operations management

The outer skin of the onion in Fig 6.2 represents the subject areas, which are usually the overall executive management processes within the organisation. These can also be referred to as prime, or Level 1 Processes.

Peel away this outer skin from the onion and a second skin is revealed, as shown in Fig 6.3.

Fig 6.3 Stripping away the outer layers reveals another layer

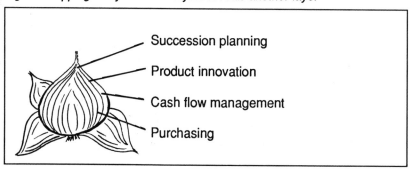

Succession planning

Product innovation

Cash flow management

Purchasing

This represents Level 2 Processes; those which are directly responsible for supporting the overall executive management processes at Level 1.

Strip away this onion skin and yet another is revealed below. This represents the Level 3 Processes which support those at Level 2 as shown in Fig 6.4.

Fig 6.4 Further peeling exposes another level

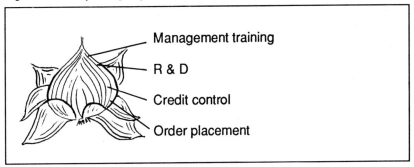

Much as the onion has successive layers of 'skin' right down to the heart, so every organisation has numerous layers of processes. It is not possible to see the next skin of the onion until the outer covering has been removed. Similarly, it is often not possible to identify the precise process to benchmark until many others have been peeled away.

Worksheet 4 for peeling the onion can be found at Appendix A

Royal Mail, for example, originally selected telephone selling as a process to benchmark. When the components of this were analysed, it was found the critical areas were: answering the phone, and ending the call.

Consequently, these two sub-processes were each investigated rather than the encompassing process of telephone selling.

It is this degree of detailed attention that is required to identify the critical process. This plays a crucial role later when selecting the benchmark.

For example, a problem for a retail bank was channelling customers, already waiting in the banking hall to be served, to the service counter smoothly and quickly. This generated a host of ideas about where to look for benchmarks, including fast-food and other service-centred organisations.

The ultimate goal is to identify, analyse, and describe individual processes, indicating where each links in to the next and who is responsible for it. A suitable analogy is completing a jigsaw. Starting with a mass of separate pieces (processes), they are gradually joined together to create a picture which resembles an organisation chart with processes instead of jobs in the boxes. Each is given a number which indicates its position in the hierarchy and builds up to a process map. (See page 85 for process maps.)

The number will depend on the complexity of the business and maturity of the organisation. Xerox Corporation in the US, for example, has identified 10 Level 1 processes with a total of 57 Level 2 processes - and these are just from the factory gate outwards! Examples at Level 1 include order fulfilment, information technology management and business management. Included at Level 2 (under order fulfilment) are:

> Order processing
> Customer service
> Product production

(under information technology management)

> Systems development
> Production systems support
> Business systems management and co-ordination

and (under business management)

> Business strategy development
> Business planning
> Business process and operations management

(This list forms just a sample of the Level 2 inclusions.)

'Business process and operations management' is further broken down into five more processes including:

> Process specification
> Benchmarking

each of which can be further broken down into its component sub-processes.

Designating process reference numbers

In the case of Xerox Corporation, a process within benchmarking would be numbered 8.3.4.x where:

8	=	The prime level 1 process reference (ie Business management which is eighth of the 10 level 1 processes)
.3	=	Number of the second level process (ie Business process and operations management)
.4	=	Number of the third level process (ie Benchmarking)
x	=	Ranking of the fourth level process (eg Process definition)

This numeric 'ranking' continues until no further associated sub-processes can be identified.

With so many processes potentially available to select for benchmarking, it is clear they must be analysed and their ranking and importance to the business prioritised. The more 'strategic' benchmarking becomes to the organisation, the more relevant this is.

Although time consuming, it becomes less so with familiarity and as the activity permeates through the company. Ideally it should be done by individuals and work groups identifying and writing up their own work processes, showing how they interlink. With the support of teams such as focus groups, quality circles or project networks gradually these can be drawn together and linked in to the total 'picture' over a reasonable period of time.

Work practices develop through custom and habit, many continuing long beyond their useful life. In the general run of business these are not questioned. However, it is often because of cumbersome or superfluous practices that jobs are complex or take longer than necessary. Pursuing simple questions like 'What/how/why do I/you do ... something?' can highlight and gradually lead to stripping out much that is unnecessary or unproductive effort. Jobs become more efficient, costs are cut, often by a surprising amount, and since nobody likes wasting time, people feel their efforts are better directed and more rewarding. Over the long term a willing attitude develops, efficiencies increase and business prospers as a result.

Analysing and understanding the process, its component parts and relationships in the total system are crucial to the success of a benchmarking exercise. The analysis has four aspects:

- ☐ Definition;
- ☐ Boundaries;
- ☐ Steps; and
- ☐ Map.

Definition

Most of us know what we mean when we describe something we are involved in. Much of the time when we talk with others we make the subconscious assumption that they share the same mental picture. If it is something which they are to become involved in this frequently leads to misinterpretation and confusion. However, it is only when things go wrong that the misunderstandings surface; what was obvious to one party was clear as mud to the other.

This highlights the need for accurate description. Never assume people 'see' things just as you do. Try the following exercise with someone you know fairly well: Describe a dream you have had recently with as much detail as you can. Ask your listener to replay the dream to you describing how they 'see' the surroundings/colours/scenery. Do these bear any resemblance to what you saw in your dream?

The process to be analysed is the one which delivers the output requiring improvement. Unless this output has been accurately defined it may prove difficult to measure or identify the process which delivers it. 'Customer Service', for example, could be the 'on-time, in-full delivery service provided to national account customers in the home market' or it might be 'answering all external telephone calls within four rings'. Knowing precisely what each output word means is vital.

Everyone understands a specific process from the perspective of how it relates to their work. This is subjective and personal. In describing it so that others may be able to understand, every detail must be included, no matter how trivial or irrelevant it may seem, thus leaving little room for ambivalence or misunderstanding.

Output definition:

If customer service is to be improved effectively, several aspects must be defined:

Customer	Who is this?
	Internal/external? National account? Top 10%/all?
	Home/overseas? Distributor/end user?
Service	What/where?
	What? Response to telephone/ technical support/complaints resolution/after-sales?
	Where? Customer premises/overseas/ reception hall?

Boundaries

When asked to describe how to make a cup of tea, cook a meal or arrange a holiday, certain initial questions require answers: 'White or black tea?', 'Sunday roast or Chinese?', 'From the point of deciding when and where to go or from contacting an agent?'.

Similarly, process start and cut-off points need to be established before moving to the next stages of analysis.

Process boundaries

What is the output of the process?
- Order filled, complaint handled, delivery made
- May be more than one; if so, check if really the same process

Who is the customer?
- The recipient of the output

What are the customer's requirements?
- How, what, when, where, why?

Is this what your process delivers?
- Not quite! Can it be improved?
- If not, is it the right process?

What are the start and end points?
- Delivery - from factory gate to shipper?

Who owns the process?
- By name, must be person responsible for improvement and with control over resources

---

Boundaries must be described precisely and clearly since they are often the root of problems or disfunctions. The more interfaces or junction points there are the greater the potential for delay and failure.

The need to define boundaries flags up whether, and how far, they extend beyond the individual, or group, responsibility (for example, where they involve more than one department or function). Where this happens, relevant others should be identified and involved.

When the boundaries have been established a named process owner should be allocated. This is someone with responsibility and control over the resources. It is preferable if they are directly involved in the process. Longer term, the owner is responsible for reviewing and monitoring best practices and ensuring that improvements continue to be made.

Process steps

Having agreed the process definition and boundaries, the next stage is to list the steps involved in the correct sequence. This means documenting what happens 'on the ground', not what is written in the manual.

Few processes are the concern of a single individual. This stage should therefore include the views of anyone with an input to, or output from, the process. Depending on the point at which they interact with it, individuals will have different ideas about what happens, when and by whom. All of these must be taken into account.

One way of dealing with the variety of views is to write the individual steps on 'Post-It' type notes which are collected together either on a board or table. When everyone is sure all the steps have been identified, they can be sorted, arranged in the correct sequence and the list drawn up.

Certainly, throughout the benchmarking process the most frequently heard phrase should be: *Hey! What do we/you/they actually mean by that?*

Moreover, this exercise may have to be repeated several times before the process is fully understood and everyone is satisfied that the final list is an accurate representation.

Worksheet 5 which lists process steps can be found at
Appendix A

Fig 6.5 Typical process steps

Process name: ....

Charted by: ....

Date: ....

Details of method process steps	Type of activity	Measurement notes
1.		....
2.		....
3.		....
4.		....
5.		....
6.		....
7.		....
8.		....
9.		....
10.		....
11.		....
12.		....
13.		....
14.		....
15.		....
16.		....

The process steps chart (Fig 6.5) has a column headed
'Measurement notes'. It is important that this be
completed as fully as possible. Even for the most simple
procedure, ascribing accurate quantitative figures leads to
clarity of current performance and targets. If undertaken
from the outset, improvements are easier to record over
time.

For some processes, such as those requiring the movement of documents or objects around the organisation, it may be helpful at this point to draw a 'flow' diagram. This is particularly useful for operations which involve a single item (an application or order form, for example) being handled by a number of people. At a glance it will be seen whether the item frequently crosses an office, department or site boundary. Significant delays and backtracking, for instance, are immediately visible.

SPEED = SIMPLICITY

When they analysed Enquiry Response Time with regard to the customer order handling process, Lucas Aerospace Ltd discovered that up to 20 ownership changes (eg release notes, export/import documentation, credit control, sales ledger) could be involved. Changes resulting from benchmarking this procedure reduced these to three. The consequent time taken to 'process' orders decreased from an average of 30 to six days (the response time requested by customers).

Conventional symbols indicate which steps involve any of five 'activities'. This picture can provide a starting point for initial improvement opportunities.

Fig 6.6 Conventional process flow symbols

O	Operation	The main 'activities in a process
⇩	Transport	Movement of people, materials, paper, information, etc.
D	Delay	Temporary storage, delay or hold-up between consecutive activities
□	Inspection	Indicates a check-point (quality or quantity)
▽	Storage	Deliberate storage, such as filing.

The example here (Fig 6.7) lists the steps involved in
making a cup of instant black tea and the resultant flow
diagram. This simplified example shows a
straightforward flow. Swings towards frequent delay or
inspection signal over-dependence on control and check
mechanisms. These create frustration and time wasting
and inevitably result in customer dissatisfaction.

Fig 6.7 Typical process steps

Process name: .. **Making a cup of instant black tea** . . . .

Charted by: .. **Oak Business Developers** . . . .

Date: ..**1 January 1992** . . . .

Details of method process steps	Type of activity	Measurement notes
1. Fill kettle	operation	1 pint
2. Boil water	op / delay	3 minutes
3. Find jar in store	op / delay	
4. Check jar contains tea	inspection	
5. Move jar to work area	operation	
6. Move cup to work area from store	operation	
7. Fetch teaspoon	operation	
8. Open jar	operation	
9. Put tea in cup	operation	1 spoon full
10. Pour on boiling water	operation	
11.		
12.		
13.		
14.		
15.		
16.		

Fig 6.8 Flow diagram for making instant tea

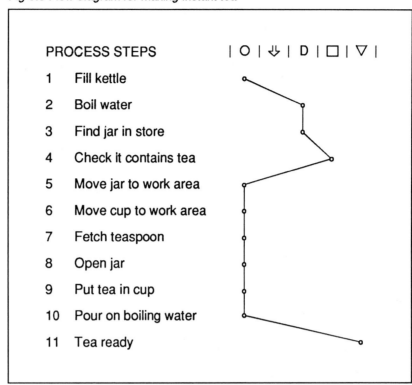

PROCESS STEPS		O	⬇	D	□	▽	
1	Fill kettle					
2	Boil water					
3	Find jar in store					
4	Check it contains tea					
5	Move jar to work area					
6	Move cup to work area					
7	Fetch teaspoon					
8	Open jar					
9	Put tea in cup					
10	Pour on boiling water					
11	Tea ready					

Process mapping

This is the final step in defining the process. The map gives an easily assimilated overview allowing the relationships, interfaces and potential failure points to be visible immediately - a significant factor when comparisons are later made with processes elsewhere. As with listing the sequential steps, the discipline involved in drawing the map prompts constant questioning and validation. Duplications and potential fail points are clearly illustrated and these can be eliminated frequently by common-sense suggestions. The resultant cost savings are often substantial.

It can be a salutary experience to map a process. The less direct is the association with it, or the smaller the input, the more bewildering the map can be. Time and again the process map proves how few people really understand the process. As with listing the steps, it is probably impossible for one person to produce a complete map. Everyone involved should be given the opportunity to contribute. This exercise provides excellent training for the teamwork necessary to facilitate subsequent improvements.

Mapping is a particularly effective way of describing complex processes. Written descriptions could run to many pages which, apart from being time consuming and tedious to read before comprehending every detail, are susceptible to misinterpretation. Later in the benchmarking exercise, when processes are compared with better practices elsewhere, documentation would be extremely cumbersome. Mapping provides a comprehensive and comprehensible means of comparison between the current and desired process and one where relevant improvements can readily be seen by everyone.

As with the flow diagrams, conventional symbols exist for process mapping which are universally recognised and so provide a 'common language' which may be understood across departmental or national boundaries.

Fig 6.9 Conventional process mapping symbols

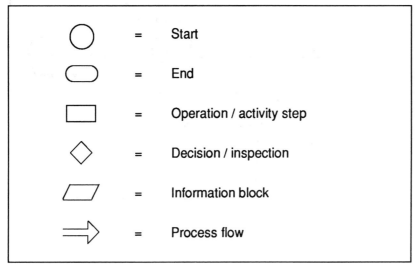

The simple tea making example given on page 85 is shown in map form. Not many work processes will be so compact! Complete walls, sometimes even rooms, may be needed for a single map with tapes connecting to outlines of inter-related processes or enlargements of specific sections.

Fig 6.10 shows a process map for making a cup of tea.

Fig 6.10 Process map for making a cup of tea

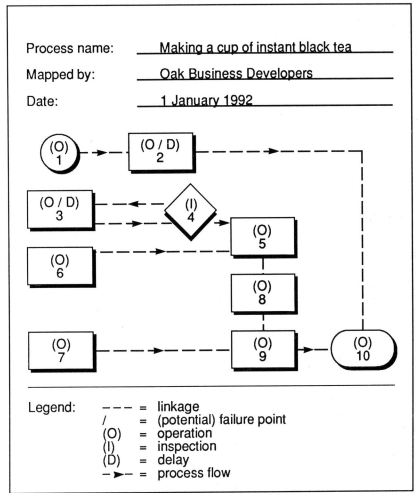

Chapter Seven

The planning stage: Partners

Contrasts with competitive analysis

Requires multi-skilled groups and

Lateral thinking and data gathering

The previous chapter examined the first two steps of the planning stage. Equally important are the two steps discussed in this chapter which lead to the eventual choice of partner.

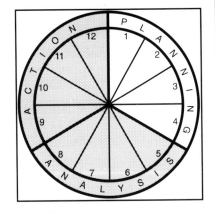

The word 'partners' is used throughout benchmarking and reflects its co-operative emphasis. This collaborative partnership concept is a contrast with competitive analyses which can be conducted without contact with, or agreement from, other companies.

STEP 3. Identify potential benchmarking partners

The following two questions provide the starting point in the search for suitable partners:

☐ Who/what is better (at the particular process) than us? And

☐ To whom is this process key for survival?

There are no instant answers or world directories of best practice but a combination of lateral thinking and organised data gathering will produce a number of options.

Assembling a multi-skill, cross-functional group to brainstorm generates more creative ideas than specialist groups. All suggestions are valid at this stage. Questions should be reserved for the end of the exercise.

WHO IS BEST?

The following is a list of some responses given by a multinational gathering of senior managers when asked which organisation they thought was the best at employing and retaining good people:

> The Armed Forces
> Airline companies
> The Secret Services
> Hewlett Packard
> Disney

At the end of the brainstorming session certain qualifying criteria must be decided which will validate and shorten the list of ideas. These will fall into a number of broad categories such as:

☐ **Language** (national and 'corporate')

☐ **Culture** (organisation and national) - it may, for instance, prove difficult for a private enterprise to make significant progress with a nationalised one

☐ **Politics** (internal, local or national)

☐ **Location** (in the example given in the box above, the Speaker was American and the answer sought was Federal Express. However, the venue was in the UK and nobody came up with this suggestion.)

☐ **Ethics**

☐ **Environmental factors**

When all these have been considered the question to answer is: Where can we look for compatible, co-operative and accessible partners?

Table 7.1 Locating benchmarking partners

INTERNAL	EXTERNAL	BEST PRACTICE
Functions / departments / at same or other location of same business / company	Other business within same group / or other company in same industry	Any company, sector or location
Advantages	**Advantages**	**Advantages**
Same language, culture systems. Ease of access to data. Existing communication channels Low threat. Good test bed for technique Relatively quick pay-back possible	Similar structure / constraints. If same group ease of access to data. Relatively low threat if in same group	May lead to signif-icant improvement. Possible high returns. May uncover break-throughs Significantly broadens corporate outlook
Drawbacks	**Drawbacks**	**Drawbacks**
Could inhibit external focus. May only give adequate returns May foster complacency	Legal / ethical considerations Potential partners may not know / understand approach Relatively long-term horizon required	Relatively difficult to gather data Long-term horizon necessary 'Best' can be controversial

Much will depend on the process chosen to benchmark. Essentially, however, there are three locations where the answer might be found:-

- ☐ Internally
- ☐ Externally
- ☐ Global best practice

Internal partners may be found in the same business and at the same or other location. This would be particularly apt if the process under the microscope were, say, telephone answering, complaints handling or document processing which are dealt with across the organisation or at a variety of points.

External partners may be located in other businesses (or countries) within the same group (such as warehousing), or from other companies within the same industry (for a non-competing process such as health and safety).

Best practice partners are selected regardless of business, industry sector or geographical location. The over-riding factor is that they have established best practice in the process under consideration. (See Table 7.1)

The learning curve in benchmarking develops from internal, through external to Best practice.

Internal partners

Most organisations start with internal comparisons wherever possible. This makes a great deal of sense since there are relatively few hurdles to overcome in terms of language, culture and data availability/accessibility. Hierarchies are understood and communication channels generally exist which make it relatively straightforward to visit or telephone someone. Depending on how far down the quality path the company is, many of the features of benchmarking will be familiar from other improvement or problem solving processes (focus groups and statistical process control for example).

Benchmarking internally provides a useful nursery slope. Within reason, any question is allowable or forgivable! Far better to learn on safe territory than a strange field. Theories, ideas and techniques can be tested and honed before subjecting them to outside challenges. Teams can develop familiarity with their own work process before going outside and seeing what others are doing. This is essential if potential for improvement is to be recognised.

Internal benchmarking can be rewarding and produce some relatively quick returns. However, it should not remain the sole form of benchmarking over an extended period. This could have negative consequences, even to the extent of rejuvenating some of the problems originally eliminated - complacency, blinkered-vision and arrogance for example.

It is crucial to maintain a balance between internal improvement and external best practice for the organisation to benefit over the longer term.

Fig 7.2 Benchmarking for growth

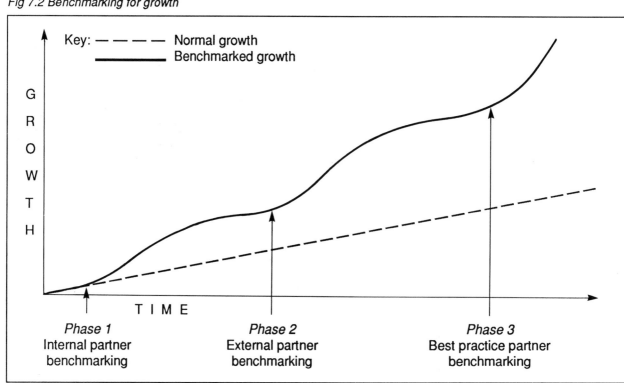

External partners

Eventually there comes a point where it is either no longer possible or desirable to improve against internal performance, or major changes (unlikely to be stimulated internally) are needed. Although external comparisons may seem more threatening, they have a higher probability of producing significant returns, discovering innovations or exploding paradigms. There is a general perception that improvements to existing processes may take longer to identify and implement if external comparisons are sought. This may be true but a single alteration or adaptation based on practice noted elsewhere could spark an innovation in your own company which revolutionises the way an operation is carried out.

The constant focus on processes gives a far wider choice of potential partners making it easy to avoid direct product competitors. Even in rare cases where they are willing to co-operate this involves the risk of industry myopia. The search is for an innovation which will give an edge over direct competitors and not one which merely makes everyone in the industry equally good. More significant perhaps is that competitor benchmarking may be perceived in the 'outside world' as collusion.

Nonetheless, there are instances where competitor benchmarking is beneficial. Processes which relate to Health & Safety or Environmental Protection and are to the general good of the global community fall into this category. Additionally, there are occasions when competitors compete in terms of product but in totally exclusive markets. Nationalised industries or those which involve highly perishable products could be included here.

> **EFFECTIVE COMPETITOR BENCHMARKING**
>
> National steel markets traditionally tend to be exclusive, one reason being that steel is expensive to ship over long distances.
>
> In seeking to improve its customer service processes, British Steel benchmarked itself against Nippon Steel in Japan. The particular focus was on Nissan Japan, to which Nippon Steel is the number one supplier. The lessons learned from this exercise helped substantially to improve British Steel's reputation with Nissan Motor Manufacturing UK.

In every external exercise, it is advisable to draw up a framework at the outset detailing the basis for proceeding. This wise precaution reduces the risk of any misunderstanding or ambiguity which could arise. The agreement should include areas/questions not open to discussion or comparison and be sensitive to each organisation's perception of its particular competitive edge. Guidelines exist for agreements between direct competitors which detail specific exclusions such as price, markets, size and share of markets etc. In most cases, strict time limits will be attached to the exercise to avoid suspicion of collusion.

Best practice partners

All benchmarking is ultimately geared to implementing innovations and improvements based on best practice. However, finding best practice can involve a long search and comparisons with it may be unrealistic if the gap is extraordinarily wide. What happens in effect, therefore, is that throughout internal and external benchmarking the search is always for measurably better practice. This provides yardsticks and milestones against which to target improvement but in the clear understanding that each is a successive step on the journey towards the best.

There is rarely a fixed point at which an organisation makes the decision to go for broke, find and then compare itself against the best. Much will depend on its performance record, how favourable this was at the outset and how much has since been improved. There are no hard and fast rules or guidelines which set down the point at which external benchmarking is finished and best practice begins. It is usually a gradual progression from better to best; the latter often only recognisable with the benefit of hindsight.

It is best practice comparisons which potentially spark improvements that provide the most significant rewards and financial returns. The first question to resolve, however, is 'What is Best?' The best car, for example, could be the fastest, cheapest, largest, most secure or adaptable and so on, depending on the selection criteria set. When looking for best practice processes it is vital to be absolutely clear of the definition of what this means for the business before beginning the search. If the search is for the best widget drilling process, first define the widget and then define drilling!

The feature which most clearly distinguishes best practice benchmarking is the creativity applied to the search for a partner. The most radical improvement ideas come from areas most would never think to look at, yet when found everyone says: 'Hey, why didn't I/we/you think of that?'

The broader the horizon the greater the likelihood that an entirely new perspective will be found. How about Undertakers for Customer Care, or Fashion Designers for Innovations or Primary Schools for Simplicity? Nor should the search be limited to the corporate world. The Apple Mackintosh computer was designed after watching the way children, not managers, learn.

SMOOTH OPERATORS

As part of its Total Quality programme, Remington Arms, a subsidiary of Du Pont in the US, conducted a customer survey. One of the 'customer needs' which featured highly in this was smoother, shinier ammunition shells.

Remington treated this seriously. Its problem was how to satisfy this need. Where could a heavy industrial manufacturer look for a process which produced smooth, polished ammunition shells? It took a long time and much lateral thought before the solution was found.

The industry sector eventually selected was cosmetics where smooth, shiny casings are produced for lipsticks. A partnership was established with Revlon and benchmarking against its practices enabled Remington Arms to make the required improvement to its ammunition shells.

When selecting potential partners:

- [ ] The partner should be measurably better

- [ ] The partner may be found: within your business at same location; other locations but same business; different businesses but same company/group; different companies but same industry; or completely outside the industry.

- [ ] Where possible avoid direct competitors, unless markets are exclusive or processes are general and affect the whole industry

- [ ] With any partner be aware of legal or ethical considerations; and draw up a procedure agreement at an early stage

- [ ] When seeking 'best' practice, define clearly what is understood by 'best' for your company or organisation.

> Worksheet 6 for selecting partners can be found at Appendix A

Step 4. Identify data sources and select appropriate method of collection

Data collection is a vital part of the benchmarking process. In particular, detailed planning is essential to ensure that attention is directed at the areas most likely to generate suitable information. The emphasis is on practicability, not academic research.

If objectives are correctly and accurately defined there is less likelihood of diversions or wasted resource. The world is full of data. It is easy to become inundated with it; the skill lies in knowing what is needed and in collecting the right, ie useful, information.

Before assigning tasks, therefore, it is useful to consider the answers to the following, which will provide a working framework:

☐ What is the *objective*?
☐ What do we *need* to look for and *why*?
☐ How *accurate* must the data be?
☐ How *much* information do we need?
☐ How *much* time and resource can we allocate to data collection - people, budgets and so on.

Responding to such questions might establish, for example, that:

☐ A maximum of three potential partners is necessary for comparison;
☐ Annual performance figures dating back three years are essential;
☐ Qualitative media/journal/trade commentary over the same three-year period would prove useful;
☐ There is no extra budget allocation and only three people working part-time can be spared for a maximum period of three months.

Using these guidelines, it is possible to plan the most appropriate search and collection methods. For example, a lack of any spare budget allocation precludes the possibility of extensive travel or mass surveys to collect information. Appropriate collection methods can be tailored accordingly. Deciding the parameters from the outset lets members of the team know precisely what the constraints are and work proceeds more efficiently.

The task of identifying sources of data is a challenging one. Depending on the selection of potential partners there will be numerous internal sources or trade associations, industry journals and analysts, surveys and company reports and so on (see Table 7.2). However, there may be less formal channels, including sources such as 'what people say'. Word of mouth recommendation can be invaluable, whether from friends or media broadcasts. No one person knows all the sources or all the answers. Gathering information is rather like piecing together a jigsaw; bits in isolation may seem meaningless but the least significant may eventually prove to be the one which completes the picture.

One strength of planning is the freedom it gives people and systems to cope with the unforeseen. A framework for data collection helps not only in collecting the obvious information but enables otherwise seemingly irrelevant details to be put in the picture. Notice how it is that when you have just bought a blue car, there are many other blue cars around? The number does not suddenly increase, merely your awareness of them. Most of the data required already exists; finding it is just a matter of opening eyes and minds and recognising the essential and the inessential.

The data collection plan should include a list of the internal and (or) external data sources to be pursued, by whom, how and when. Responsibility for collection should be assigned to a named person wherever possible. There are two reasons for this:

Table 7.2 Typical sources of data

INTERNAL	EXTERNAL
Company library	External libraries
Corporate publications	Special reports/surveys
Databases	External databases
Internal surveys	Media broadcasts/reports
Market research	Trade shows/journals
Personal networks	Professional networks
Planning documents	Seminars/conferences
Financial documents	Industry experts/analysts
	Finance houses
	Suppliers/customers
	Company reports
	Business schools/academia
	Consultants
	Trade associations
	Professional institutes

Firstly, the exercise may continue over an extended period. If a name is attached to each specific element of data collection there is greater likelihood of the work being handed over when someone is promoted or moved prior to the end of the exercise. Secondly, it is far easier and more natural for others, whether in the team or not, to communicate or identify with a name than a job title.

The data collection plan should detail the methods by which it is to be collected (for example, by telephone call or survey, personal interview, questionnaire, library visit etc). This provides information for others (not necessarily just members of the team) in the short term and a useful reference if the benchmarking exercise is repeated at a later date.

Wherever possible, full details should be included in records of the planning process. This is time consuming and there will inevitably be a temptation to skip some details which 'seem obvious' at the time. What is obvious from one perspective can, however, be obscure from another and clear, comprehensive documentation is always invaluable.

DON'T DUMP DOCUMENTATION

A bank was faced with major recession in the three areas to which it was most heavily exposed. Profits tumbled. Drastic measures were required to ensure its continued existence.

One initiative introduced as part of a wide ranging business improvement strategy was 'best methods' harmonisation. This involved considerable investment over several years and involved key practices in branches across the world. Central to this was detailed analysis of all essential business processes.

The eventual turnaround effected through the improvement strategy became legendary in the industry. Time passed. Staff moved on. Years later, as part of another initiative, processes again came under the microscope. But much of the documentation from the previous exercise had been lost in the intervening period. What could have been a relatively straightforward updating task became instead a major undertaking.

A precise date (day, month and year) by which the information is to be collected should be included in the plan. Vague schedules, such as 'mid-July', 'end of Quarter 4', are insufficient and open to abuse. When each stage is complete it should be signed off, dated and other team members advised. This is particularly important since it may impact on the work other team members are doing.

When all the planned data have been collected analysis can begin to determine whether the potential partners originally listed are still relevant, whether others have been revealed or no suitable partners can be found.

> Worksheet 7 for planning data collection can be found at Appendix A

Chapter Eight

The analysis stage

Select the best team

Adhere to the original plan

Balance data collection

A fundamental difference between the planning and analysis stages of benchmarking is that whereas the former is best carried out sequentially - the results of one step determining the course of the next - steps 5 to 8 are iterative and can be carried out at the same time. This is due not only to the nature of the work involved but all teams work in different ways, depending on the mix of skills and strengths represented. What matters in the end is that all the steps are carried out diligently.

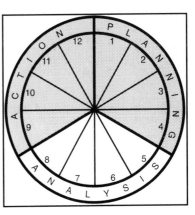

Table 8.1 Members of the benchmark team

A 'typical' benchmarking team comprises:

Leader
(who may be the same person as ...)
Process owner
+
Representation of the following:
- Analytical skills
- Work process documentation skills
- Information search and analysis capability
+
Where and if appropriate
Customer (internal and/or external)

Step 5.   Collecting data and selecting partners

In Step 4 the data collection exercise was planned, resources allocated and responsibilities and methods assigned. This next step is concerned with carrying out this plan, analysing the data and determining whether they confirm or dismiss the potential partners selected at Step 3.

Whether all, or selected, members of the team are involved in both collection and analysis will depend on the composition of the group. A typical team should include good analytical skills and information search capability - this could involve one or all members.

However many of the team are involved, it is important to adhere to the plan, particularly in respect of the completion/review timings. When analysing information the temptation is to feel that more data would provide a clearer picture. However, more does not necessarily help, even though yet more could, perceptually, make all the difference. Data collected under such circumstances stand a good chance of becoming increasingly spurious or misleading. One reason for fixing time limits to the exercise is to concentrate minds on essentials. Irrelevant and 'nice to know' data should be ruthlessly discarded.

Analysis will determine either that it is worthwhile pursuing one or more of the original potential partners; or that none on the original list are of use. In the second case it will be necessary to return to Step 3 and short-list other candidates in the light of what has been discovered. Assuming, however, that there were several potential partners at least one of these should prove worthy of closer analysis and this, more often than not, will require a visit to the company.

Preparing a visit to a potential benchmark partner

The visit should be the conclusive port of call for information. Unlike competitive analyses, the essence is to comprehend *how* practices result in superior performance. To understand the combination of skills, attitudes, values, pride and culture which motivate people to produce excellent results it is necessary to experience them at first hand. At least one visit must be made to 'get a feel' for how things are done there.

Benchmarking is still relatively new and it should not be assumed that the partner company will understand the technique, the work involved or potential benefits. Whether or not a relationship already exists the initial contact should be carefully thought through. Some useful questions to consider before this include:

- Do we know this company?
- Who do we know in this company?
- With whom do we need to establish contact? (Title, level etc)
- How can we clearly explain the purpose of the contact?
- Who is the best person in our organisation for this task?

Once this ground has been covered, and before an approach is made, some time should be given to planning a visit in outline. The more carefully this is thought through, the more convincingly it will communicate and strengthen any resulting association. Questions, shown in Table 8.2, need to be covered at this stage:

Table 8.2 Questions to consider when preparing a visit

What	-	Is the objective?
Why	-	Did you choose this partner?
What	-	Is in it for them?
What	-	Process do you wish to see?
Where	-	Do you wish to visit? (Business/site/ plant)
Who	-	Is/are the key person/s?
When	-	Is it best to visit?
How	-	Many people (your team and theirs) will need to be involved?
How	-	Long is the envisaged visit (hours/ days?)

When these have been addressed contact can be made and the visit arranged. Depending on the degree of experience or awareness of benchmarking in the proposed partner company it may be relevant to arrange an initial meeting to explain what is being undertaken and why. Although much of benchmarking is a combination of familiar tools from other performance improvement approaches, the philosophy that underpins it is counter-cultural to the behaviour of some traditional organisations. During the initial approach, therefore, the co-operative element should be stressed, including any mutual benefits which could result, a readiness to share any information gathered and the lessons to be learned.

There are no formal 'visiting' rules but a general Code of Conduct has developed based on maintaining an honest, courteous and respectful manner in benchmark dealings. If there is a guiding principle it is: *'Do as you would be done by'*.

Table 8.3 The search for information

When seeking information:

☐ Be honest and open about your purpose

☐ Do not misrepresent yourself or your company

☐ Never ask for something you would not be happy to give in return if asked

☐ Offer and be prepared to sign a confidentiality agreement

☐ Agree from the outset any information which may not be requested (particularly if benchmarking with competitors)

☐ Offer and be prepared to share findings with the partner(s)

The groundwork complete, preparations can be made for the visit. Thoroughly completing this beforehand allows a focus on 'looking and learning' on site. Preparation should include the following:

☐ Understand fully what is being sought and consider the questions which may need to be asked. (It is helpful to write an aide memoir and/or a self-prompt questionnaire which the team members can refer to during the visit.)

☐ Take the correct people on the visit. This should always include the process owner but it is wise also to take an informed 'observer' who will see and hear objectively.

☐ Assess hidden values and obtain a feel for what is essential. Be sure to include people with empathy and good listening skills in the visit team.

To make best use of time available during the visit, send the host company details of the areas and topics of interest for analysis and discussion. This allows the host to have the relevant information to hand and field the most suitable people for the meeting.

The purpose of the visit is to gather details of the practices which are in place and understand how tasks are completed. In rare instances the difference between your approach to a process and that of the host will be visible immediately. A tour of the plant may reveal a revolutionary piece of loading equipment, for example. More often, however, performance differences depend on a combination of subtle factors.

Ask for quantitative data to substantiate what is happening, but avoid the temptation to information graze. It is easy to be side-tracked or overwhelmed by novelty; adhere rigidly to the plan and you are still likely to come away with more ideas than you bargained for!

By the end of the visit the team should feel confident of being able to assess the blend of factors which effects superior performance at the host company. For complex processes, more than one visit may be necessary to complete the picture.

Table 8.4 Attitudes during the visit

During the visit
☐ The question uppermost in the mind should be 'how' is this done?
☐ Focus attention on matters of immediate concern. Do not succumb to information grazing
☐ If what is seen or heard is not understood - ask
☐ Consciously try to feel behind the visible for the hidden attitudes/skills/ values which provide vital clues to superior performance

On rare occasions, despite evidence of better practices and processes, it may be impracticable to proceed to benchmarking with a company that has been visited. The reason could be that the cultures are too dissimilar: maybe the quality programme in one company is too far ahead of the other; or one is part of a multinational group whilst the other is a small private company or recently de-nationalised. If signs of potential culture clash or language barriers are apparent either in the early stages of the visit or subsequent negotiations, it is preferable to agree not to pursue the matter. Mutually rewarding partnerships rarely develop where values are unevenly matched.

After the visit the most immediate task is to document the facts and perceptions gathered. The sooner this is done the better because even overnight the initial ideas, perceptions and feelings will be subtly influenced by the subconscious. Xerox Corporation teams, for example, write their report immediately following the visit, regardless of what time of day that may be. It is far better to use the facilities of a hotel near to the benchmark company than wait for everyone to meet in the office next day.

The task should not be delegated to any single member of the visit team. Each person will have a view that is valuable. Before compiling the final draft of the visit report all members should contribute these - maybe during a brainstorm-type session - at the group's meeting point. Of particular importance to note are key, or frequently repeated, words which may provide the clues to superior performance.

There are four key areas which should be covered in the report.

☐ Differences in process: These are the practices involved in performing the actual process.

☐ Differences in management: These are the differences which apply across the range of systems and support practices, such as staffing, skill levels, shift type and number, and resource allocation.

☐ Differences in structure: This includes the nature of the organisation; whether it is a private or public company, centralised or decentralised for example. It also includes location (city centre or suburban) and age of structural facilities etc. whichwill influence the level and type of costs incurred.

☐ Differences in culture: This embodies 'the way things are done around here'. Management may be autocratic, paternalistic or participative. Doors may be open or firmly closed. First names may predominate or titles be 'de rigeur'. The atmosphere could be cool, courteous and professional; warm, vibrant and entrepreneurial; or cold, studious and exclusive.

A well-written visit report performs a vital role during later communications. It complements other desk research data with 'live' facts. These provide a human dimension to staff presentations, for example, or anecdotal material for internal publications or wider media use. One good factual report of better performance can win over more sceptics than a host of metrics. Depending on the degree of support for change internally, it may be useful to 'float' the report in front of a devil's advocate or band of disbelievers. This will provide the opportunity to see the findings through other people's eyes. Arguments, explanations and descriptions can be tested before presenting them to one or more of the ultimate decision makers.

Step 6.   Determine the gap compared to the benchmark

The prime objective during the visit is to complement and/or validate data collected from other sources in order to establish causes of performance difference between your organisation and the benchmark company. A visit also ensures that like is being compared with like. Siting and size of plant, number of filling lines, physical structures and so on will be obvious immediately. Whilst collecting data prior to the visit assumptions will have been made (an accounting system may define a month as 28 or 30 days or a calendar month for example); these could be overturned completely by witnessing another procedure first hand.

To determine the gap, information must be compiled to provide the basis for analysis and measurement. 'What gets measured gets improved.' Activities must be measurable before they can stimulate change. The methods chosen for measuring the gap between the existing and the superior performance should reflect the on-going, long-term nature of benchmarking. The aim should be for clarity and simplicity so that measures will be sustainable and capable of interpretation even by those not involved with the exercise.

It is equally essential to select a practical number of appropriate measures. The diagram below shows those derived by one company following rigorous analysis of its situation. These provided the basis for benchmarking.

Fig 8.1 *One example of benchmark architecture*

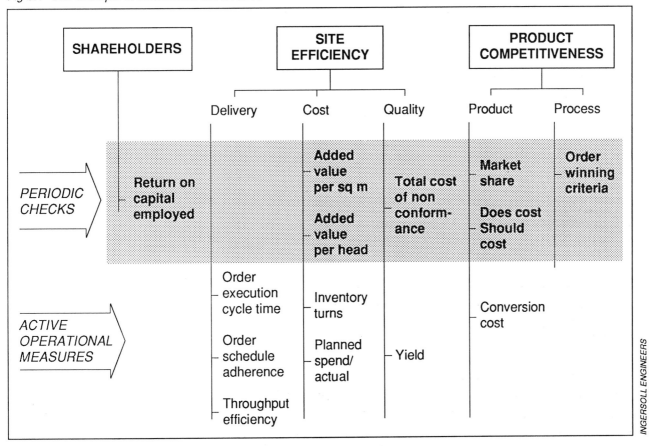

'Hard' quantitative differences are relatively straightforward to identify or calculate. Figures can be displayed graphically using standard analysis models, such as pie charts, bar charts, histograms and so on.

Table 8.5 *Analysing performance*

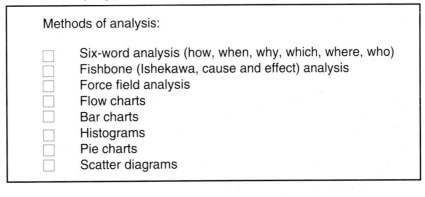

Any system or activity conducted by an enterprise can be described by a simple process model, such as the one below. Measurements can be made at certain points:

- ☐ The input stage
- ☐ During the work process or activity
- ☐ The output stage
- ☐ On the results
- ☐ On the feedback loop

Fig 8.2 Process measurement points

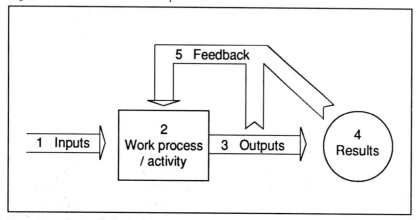

Depending on the process in question measurements may be taken from one or more of these points. For example, customer service could be observed at:

Point 1   -   Stock in warehouse
Point 3   -   Accuracy of delivery
Point 5   -   The customer's perception of service

Good benchmarking combines measurement of quantitative and qualitative data. A means of deriving numeric comparisons from visual or perceptual information is, therefore, required to determine what else accounts for performance gaps. For each intangible comparison, such as 'better working atmosphere' or 'more satisfied customers' indicators can be found from which numeric outputs are derived.

Where these are not immediately obvious a numeric interpretation may be found by returning to the previous step. Most of the intangible information will flow from points 4 (Results) and 5 (Feedback) and suitable measures will often be found at 3(Outputs). In some cases, however, it may be necessary to go back as far as 1 (Inputs) to find a 'measurable' factor.

Fig 8.3 Measurement factors

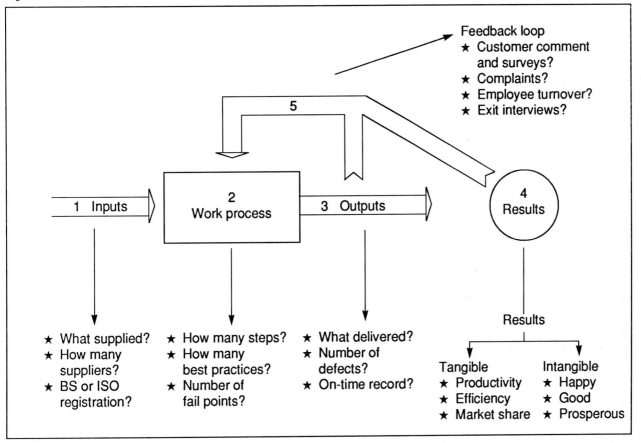

No matter how obscure the qualitative information, measurables can always be found by this back-tracking mechanism. Some of the indicators will be more apt or useful than others. Initially it is best to list as many as possible and gradually draw out and emphasise the few which are most meaningful.

OUTPUT INDICATORS OF QUALITATIVE PERFORMANCE

Good working atmosphere: Gaps could be established by measuring:

- ☐ Labour turnover over a fixed period
- ☐ Reward and recognition systems (levels/ frequency/reviews)
- ☐ Off-site or on-the-job training per person per year (days/spend)
- ☐ Number/variety of shared social events
- ☐ Employee well-being initiatives (canteen/ healthcare etc)

Satisfied customers: Gaps could be established by measuring:

- ☐ Number/type of complaints
- ☐ Number of repeat orders
- ☐ Technical back-up (team/specific initiatives)
- ☐ Average 'age' of customer relationships
- ☐ Special promotion packages (number/type)

Once suitable measures have been established the gap analysis can be produced. This should be an objective assessment of the size and nature of the performance difference. Gaps are referred to as POSITIVE when the *internal* practices produce a *better* performance than comparative ones; or NEGATIVE when the *internal* practices produce a *worse* performance than comparative ones.

In the early stages, most gaps will be negative. However, when benchmarking is the norm or reaches a stage of maturity within the organisation, some may be positive. This is quite feasible. It is possible that a component of a process, internally considered capable of improvement, is nonetheless better than that of the partner. This will not necessarily be apparent until the analysis is carried out. Experience indicates that this quite commonly occurs and leads to positive benefit for the partner, who will be able to improve that part of his process. Sometimes a joint decision is taken to seek a 'best practice' third party comparison for this element. This then forms the basis of a separate exercise (and incidentally accounts for development of benchmarking networks).

Also, as programmes roll through the organisation, there will be knock-on improvements on performance areas not formally benchmarked. These will be recognised only when attention is focused on them.

Whether the bias is negative or positive, the gap analysis should include:

- [ ] Tables providing descriptive and numeric data on both benchmark and existing processes
- [ ] A calculation of the size of the gap
- [ ] An explanation of the most feasible possible causes
- [ ] An assessment of the scope/nature of changes which would be required to close the gap, and exceed the benchmark performance
- [ ] Priority of these to produce optimum improvement
- [ ] Evaluation of suitability/practicability of implementation
- [ ] Time-frame and cost assessment
- [ ] Conclusions and recommendations
- [ ] A graphic illustration of the performance gap

Fig 8.4 Displaying the performance gap

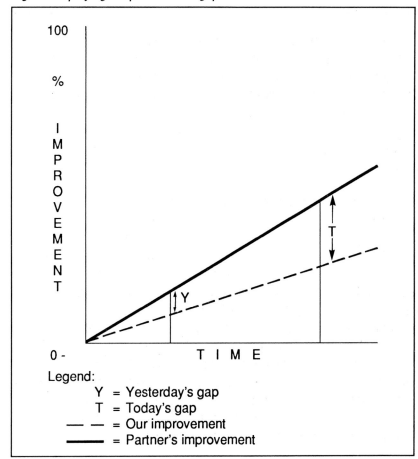

Legend:
Y = Yesterday's gap
T = Today's gap
— — = Our improvement
—— = Partner's improvement

The gap analysis is fundamental to the later communications plan (see Step 9) and should avoid use of jargon or hyperbole. The graphic display should be clear, uncluttered and capable of interpretation across all levels of the organisation.

Step 7. Establish differences in process

The experience of mapping out your process will be invaluable during this step.

The clearest and most comprehensive way to highlight differences is by direct visual comparison. It would be an extraordinary stroke of luck to find that a map of the benchmark process already exists at the partner company. It is more likely that your team will have to draw it. For complex processes, numerous discussions may be necessary before it is complete. However, it is essential to have as comprehensive a picture as possible and there is nothing to be gained from short-circuiting this procedure.

When complete, the map can be displayed side by side with that of the existing process, preferably close to where the process takes place. The differences should be clearly highlighted. A third map can then be drawn depicting clearly the alterations or adjustments and how the process will look following integration of these. Where only minor alterations are to be made it is easier to draw enlarged versions of those sections which will be affected rather than the whole.

The maps should be accompanied by a documentary synopsis of the changes together with the dates when they are to be implemented and completed.

While the maps will show the actual process differences and alterations, the most difficult elements to differentiate will be those associated with the intangible factors. Attitude, paradigm and culture differences cannot be shown on the map nor can they be adopted wholesale. For this reason documenting what was seen and felt promptly following the visit is vital. There may be key concepts or factors which could be incorporated in other on-going quality or training initiatives to secure longer term improvement. An indication of these, or any other knock-on effects of the benchmarking visit, should be included on the synopsis.

Fig 8.5 Displaying the processes

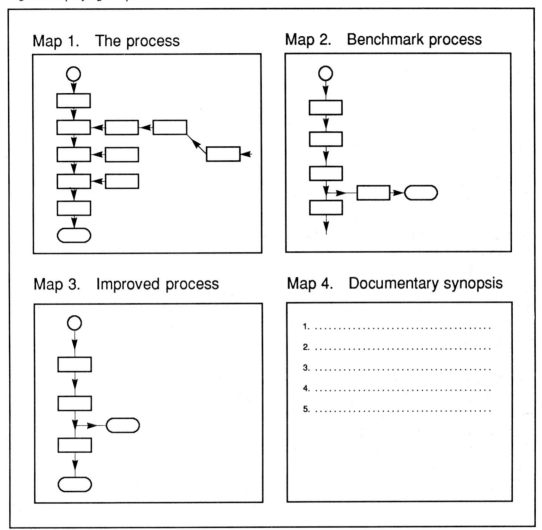

Map 1. The process

Map 2. Benchmark process

Map 3. Improved process

Map 4. Documentary synopsis

1. ....
2. ....
3. ....
4. ....
5. ....

Step 8. Target future performance

Having graphically displayed the gap in performance (Step 6) this now needs to be extrapolated forward to plan future performance. However, traditional target setting is inappropriate and insufficient in today's dynamic environment. Whatever difference now exists between the best practice and any other, will expand through momentum even if the best practice company does nothing extra. Since best practice rarely occurs without conscious effort it is probable that companies achieving it will continue to improve at an ever increasing rate rather than standing still.

Displaying the future position, both conservatively and potentially, will help in setting targets which take the company to a position of superiority in its industry. It is impossible to know precisely what will happen in time to come, but a scenario based on the impact of reasonable assumptions can be illustrated.

WHEN CALCULATING THE GAP

☐   Never make assumptions about the future based purely on the past or present - allow for what may happen tomorrow

☐   To make up for the present gap, the rate of improvement over the target period must be greater than the benchmark partner's

☐   But the benchmark partner's rate of improvement will also increase even if it does nothing extra

---

This suggests that targets set for your company's future performance must be well beyond the current gap. The reaction they provoke should be one of incredulity rather than speculation.

Key points to bear in mind are:

☐ The gap exists because performance varies
☐ Only past and present performance can be known
☐ Extrapolating historic performance forward inevitably expands the gap at the same rate
☐ The poorer performer, being behind from the outset, must increase the rate of improvement by a greater amount than the better performer just to maintain the gap
☐ The better performer is likely to improve at an increasing rate
☐ So the poorer performer must make a significant improvement leap in order to close the gap
☐ Which means that to leap ahead, the poorer performer must improve by an amount which represents the initial lag, plus the performance difference today, plus an estimate of the future potential gap plus an extra contingency figure to allow for major breakthroughs at the benchmark company over the projected period.

'We already have enough ideas in place to double our rate of improvement over the next five years.'
(Chairman: Toyota)

It is essential, therefore, to set targets beyond those achieved by the benchmark company since it will not stand still. Even in the time it takes to complete the analysis, your partner may already have moved ahead.

Fig 8.6 Assessing future performance

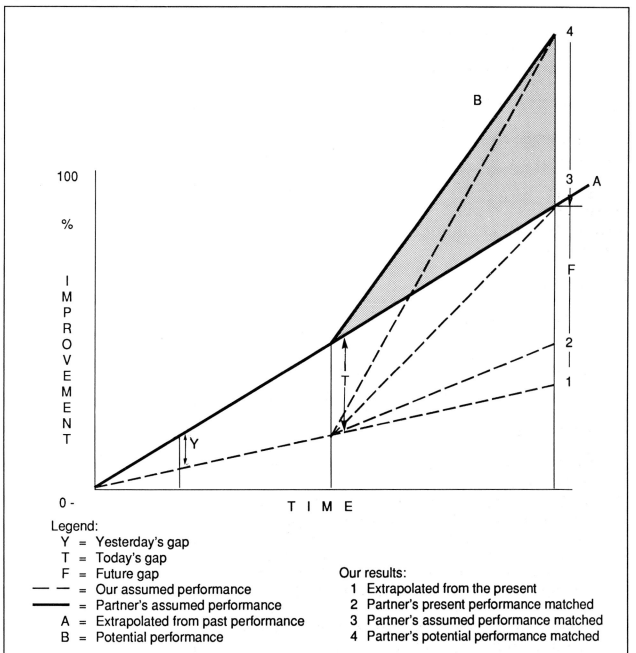

Legend:
Y = Yesterday's gap
T = Today's gap
F = Future gap
— — = Our assumed performance
———— = Partner's assumed performance
A = Extrapolated from past performance
B = Potential performance

Our results:
1 Extrapolated from the present
2 Partner's present performance matched
3 Partner's assumed performance matched
4 Partner's potential performance matched

Chapter Nine

The action stage

Communication is essential

Follow through determines success

Monitor progress and update

IT IS in this stage that information and knowledge gathered during planning and analysis is converted into efforts which will result in improved performance. This is not guaranteed. A manual can, at best, describe only what should be done if achievement is to have a chance. It is the diligent follow through which determines success, or otherwise, of the programme.

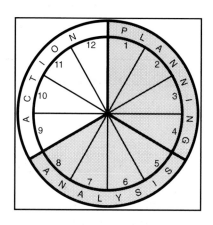

Planning and analysis are largely passive activities involving relatively few people; it is possible to halt the exercise temporarily or permanently at any stage with little deleterious effect. Conversely, the further the programme rolls into the action stage, the more difficult it is to stop. It is similar to pressing the emergency switch on a moving train; the train speeds up as it moves out of the station and the greater the distance travelled the more serious the effects will be.

Without exception, all managers pro-active in benchmarking stress the importance of total commitment. This must be demonstrated by all those involved in the exercise. However, it is at the Action stage that senior management commitment is particularly crucial if large-scale resources or changes are required.

This, therefore, is the vital ingredient for success during stage 3. All action plans should be formulated in the context of gaining and sustaining wholehearted commitment.

The action steps, as in stage 2, are iterative. Moreover, since many of them will have a resultant, often on-going ripple effect through the organisation, it is essential to ensure regular monitoring and up-dating mechanisms are built in from the outset.

The more positive and efficient the execution of introductory action steps, the greater will be the potential for improvement over the longer term.

Step 9. Communicate benchmark findings

As Chapter Three indicates, benchmarking can be instrumental in promoting the climate for change. It is, however, only one of a series of initiatives which can be employed to effect broad reform. With any Total Quality or Change programme, whether or not consequent action plans are adopted, smooth progress depends on communication. Carefully planned and sensitively executed, it can secure commitment and gain co-operation.

People are naturally resistant or reluctant to adopt new practices and this must be overcome before implementation. The first stage of the communication programme, prior to introducing any new initiatives, should cascade the background and findings of the benchmarking exercise through the organisation to gain this commitment. Belief in the need for change and the willingness to undertake it will be much enhanced if people receive a clear, positive message.

It is probable in the early stages that only those directly involved with the exercise will know or understand what has been happening. Communications should therefore provide detailed reasons for benchmarking as well as opportunities, plans and objectives for the future. Where practicable, visual aids, such as posters (for information not exhortation), should be used to support and highlight key points. Many companies have notice boards (mostly ignored when they contain only close-written pages on procedures and policies) which are ideal for punchy bullet-point messages. Audio tapes provide an effective medium for people whose work involves slugs of 'spare' learning time in cars (sales and technical service staff for example).

The consequences of benchmarking will be most keenly felt by those whose jobs are directly affected. In addition to a carefully constructed general communications programme, particular attention should be focused on these individuals or groups.

When designing the communications programme it is important to consider:

☐   Who is most affected by what has been discovered?

☐   How will this affect them?

Everyone reacts differently to the prospect of change; some people welcome the challenge, others feel uncomfortable or apprehensive about its effects while a minority strongly resist it. Communications must be sympathetic and appeal to the whole range of feeling. Strong resistance can sometimes be overcome by involving the person or people in a visit to the benchmark company. On witnessing better practice the resentment associated with being told something better can be achieved is often dissolved. This is particularly so if the result of improving the work is seen to be making it cleaner, simpler, or more enjoyable; as well as more efficient.

> **BUZZ GROUPS!**
>
> When people, systems and companies are working well and achieving excellent results they exude a positive, often contagious, energy. The 'buzz' varies from stimulating to inspirational! One company, before involving any new people in its benchmarking programme, regularly sends them on a tour of the partner company's premises. The objective is to 'feel and see' at first hand the atmosphere and conditions which exist when work is being done to the best of people's ability. Described as 'rolling the last few feet of a suspense film first' they maintain that this provides the extra impetus and inspiration needed to cope with any difficulty, disruption and drama along the journey to improvement.

Co-operation is the second requirement in bringing about change; extraordinary amounts may be essential to achieve superior performance. In addition to securing commitment, therefore, the communications programme should prepare the basis for teamwork and collaboration. The exact nature of this will depend on the culture and style of the organisation. An effective programme will, however, include consideration of key factors listed below.

Communications should include:

- [ ] A vision of the future;
- [ ] What benchmarking is and how it fits in with this;
- [ ] The benefits to be gained;
- [ ] Why benchmarking is being implemented;
- [ ] Which process is being examined and why;
- [ ] The name of the process owner(s);
- [ ] How and why the benchmark partners were selected; and
- [ ] The quantitative and qualitative benchmarks.

Communications should also address the following issues:

☐ What are the benefits to the individual?
☐ What is the goal?
☐ What is the time frame?
☐ Who will be involved?
☐ Why and when will they be involved?
☐ How will they be involved?

All too often, new initiatives run out of steam after the initial flurry of activity. Life settles back to normal and inertia creeps in. Renewed injections of enthusiasm and support are required to prevent this. Progress must be reported regularly and on a recurring basis - not just when spectacular strides are made - so that everyone can share in the achievement.

Such reports should encompass:

☐ Which milestones have been reached;
☐ What has been accomplished so far (factual and anecdotal);
☐ What the next milestones are; and
☐ Review of targets (especially if these have been altered in any way).

Once the concept and practice of benchmarking have been accepted internally, the communications programme should broaden to include external 'listeners'. Whilst some managers may be reluctant, good benchmarking companies talk openly and keenly about their experience and progress. AT&T in the US go further by offering its benchmarking workshops to the general public.

Seminars and conferences provide excellent opportunities for dissemination of experiences as well as for encouraging potential benchmark partners. A senior North American executive with Digital Equipment Corporation regularly gives benchmarking presentations at international conferences. At each, he invites members of the audience to drop their business cards in a strategically positioned box if they wish to know more about the subject generally or networks in particular.

Similar initiatives may broaden the external perception of managers whilst multiplying the number of channels for new ideas to flow into the organisation.

Step 10. Adjust goals and develop corrective improvement plan

Incremental improvement can be achieved using the old remedies. Quantum leaps forward require the strength of purpose to go for bold goals, which are rarely attained without discomfort or even an amount of pain. Sometimes this is coupled with an extraordinary leap of faith.

THE LIGHT FANTASTIC!

Nissan Motor set a bold goal for its bulb suppliers: maximum of one defect in 10m within seven years. At the time the industry average defect rate was 1 per 100.

However, Nissan did not disclose its ultimate goal from the outset. Selecting its best bulb supplier (Philips) it set it the target of one defect per 1,000. When this was achieved, it moved the goal post to one per 10,000; then one per 100,000; then one per million. Each time Nissan moved the goal, no matter how impossible it seemed, Philips was determined to reach it until the final one in 10m was achieved.

Everyone was delighted, especially Philips. When Nissan disclosed that this had been its goal from the outset, Philips' managers asked how the Japanese company had known it could be possible. 'You were our best supplier of bulbs so we knew that if anyone could do it you could, even though we didn't know how you were going to get there' came the reply!

It is this order of faith which accompanies bold goals.

As in this example, once the strategy is formulated, a plan to achieve it must be developed. It is easy to underestimate our, and other people's potential; drawing out the best is usually only possible through a combination of vision - to recognise potential and patience - to nurture its development. First teach people to climb, then ask them to scale the north face of the Eiger!

The more ambitious the goal, the more flexible that initial target must be. The unique feature of benchmarking is the comparison with actual 'best practice' performance. This gives a realistic reflection of what is ultimately, if not immediately, achievable.

Adjusting the goals requires setting milestones commensurate with people's ability; at the same time providing realistic yardsticks which stretch but do not break them. Individuals need and respond to challenges. However, they buckle or rebel if asked to undertake the impossible without the requisite tools, or the freedom to enable ingenuity to find a way. The more effort that is demanded, or responsibility devolved, the greater the support, training and guidance needed.

The achievement of goals does not depend solely on the willingness or skill of individuals. Goals must be sufficiently flexible to allow for continual minor adjustment in the light of new information. This may result from extrinsic factors such as fluctuations in the political climate or feedback from customers, or intrinsically from leadership changes, inconsistencies in performance or changing budgetary considerations. Goals should constantly be synchronised to such feedback to ensure they remain realistic.

Excellent contingency planning and information management are the hallmarks of best practice; equally, they are undoubtedly major components in attaining landmark goals!

At the same time it is important to implement a corrective improvement plan. This is:

> A solution or change suggested by data collection and analysis;
> plus:
> A plan to implement the change or solution;
> plus:
> A method to monitor/check/review impact on outputs, results and critical success factors.

The corrective improvement plan is the set of actions to effect the solution. It incorporates the means to review and monitor progress towards the goal, and the impact of benchmarking activities on critical success factors.

It is crucial to identify and secure the commitment of those whose support is essential in the early stages of implementation. Additionally, this momentum must be maintained over the longer term. There is a difference between:

☐ Active commitment, which is required from those involved in carrying out the improvements, and

☐ Passive commitment from those who must be relied on to provide essential background support (such as sanctioning expenditure).

Successful implementation will stand or fall according to the degree of engagement of all these people.

Essential check questions to ask before formulating the improvement plan are:

☐ Is the collated information comprehensive and accurate?
☐ Can it be trusted?
☐ Are the benchmarked processes measurably better?
☐ Are the changes necessary to improve existing practices commensurate with the available ability?
☐ Do the changes accord with existing values?

The answers must always be positive. Assuming this is so, the task must be to generate the optimum plan and implementation procedures. Where necessary, (for example where capital expenditure is needed) these should include securing relevant approvals.

There are no golden rules for procedure. The way things are done will be influenced by prevailing attitudes and culture. However, the following suggests some general guidelines.

Corrective improvement plan - general guidelines

- ☐ Decide on the criteria which will be used to judge solutions;
- ☐ Balance long term solutions with short term gain;
- ☐ Generate as many solutions as possible and as many potential reasons why they might fail;
- ☐ Select the most appropriate solution;
- ☐ Agree master implementation and monitoring plan;
- ☐ Split into manageable steps with built-in contingency;
- ☐ Identify whose (active and passive) commitment is required;
- ☐ Communicate clearly to everyone involved;
- ☐ Agree and draw up individual Action Plans* for those directly involved in implementation - these should incorporate unambiguous goals and deadlines;
- ☐ Set up an uncomplicated monitoring and reporting system; and
- ☐ Ensure everyone clearly understands the process, evaluation criteria and communication lines applicable when these are achieved.

Worksheet 8 showing a sample action plan can be found at Appendix A

Step 11. Implement corrective improvement plan

No amount of reading, writing or exhortation will secure successful implementation. There are no quick fixes or easy answers, no magic wands or secret solutions. There is only the guarantee that the accolade of 'best' will not be achieved through one solitary action.

Two factors, however, which can help determine success are: detailed attention and attention to detail!

When all the hype is stripped away from the debate about what made Japanese firms pre-eminent, their obsession with detail is one common denominator which stands out.

Assuming that communications strategies have established secure foundations, attention to detail will be the one factor which governs the outcome of any implementation plan. A question which frequently occupies the mind of would-be benchmarkers is how an already excellent company can stay ahead if everyone else is benchmarking against it. (The implication being that their methods then become just average.) The truth is that whilst many seek and find best practice, few companies are sufficiently adept in detailed, attentive follow-through to overtake the leaders. Furthermore, outstanding performers are rarely complacent. They continue to hone their competitive edge and so increase their potential for staying in front.

During implementation attention should be focused on:

- ☐ The process being improved; and
- ☐ Progress of the improvement plan.

In Step 7 (Establish differences in process) maps were drawn showing the differences between the existing and the best practice processes and highlighting the changes required. During implementation the desired changes should be effected in the agreed sequence and carefully monitored. Major changes should be implemented on a reduced (test) basis for a period and only scaled up when success is proved. For example, when initiating major accounting system changes, these could be trialled at one location before being implemented across the company. The general procedure is:

- ☐ Try out the new process for the planned (or test) period;
- ☐ Monitor and measure results to determine whether the change is working;
- ☐ Document all changes;
- ☐ Communicate initial results;
- ☐ Plan further improvement;
- ☐ Implement and monitor;
- ☐ Document; and
- ☐ Communicate.

When all the planned changes are in place, redraw the final process map and display it in a suitably prominent place.

Fig 10.1 The route for successful improvement

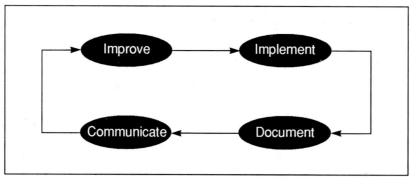

Monitoring progress during the improvement plan must allow for the unforeseen as well as the planned agenda.

This means:

☐ Maintaining the commitment of everyone affected by or involved in implementation. Most programmes will take at least weeks, if not months, to implement and over this time enthusiasm is bound to wane if not constantly fuelled by success stories (no matter how small), praise and other signs of recognition and appreciation.

☐ Frequent and enthusiastic communication of progress and achievements throughout the organisation

☐ Review of contingency plans and deadlines

☐ Modifying the plan as suggested by unforeseen or unexpected developments

☐ Constant monitoring and review of progress

☐ Concise and precise documentation of improvements

When the benchmark goal has been achieved ...

TELL THE WORLD!

then ...

SET BOLDER GOALS!

Step 12.   Review progress and calibrate

Review is to benchmarking as breathing is to life. It is so obviously necessary that it is often taken for granted. Many people only breathe efficiently and effectively when they are made aware of bad habits; shallow breathing, for example, can compound the effects of tiredness or stress whereas deep breathing helps combat them.

Similarly with review. It is essential but how many people have a disciplined procedure? The necessity for this, in the context of the overall benchmarking process, is discussed in detail in the following chapter. However, since it is also the concluding step in each exercise it is covered briefly here.

During the 12-step process there is a number of points at which it is advisable to take an objective look at progress. In Step 5 for instance, where, if no partner is found, several or all of the previous steps must be recycled.

The final review at Step 12 has a different quality. The main question to be raised is:

> 'Have we met our objectives for this benchmarking exercise?'

If the review procedure has been thorough during successive stages then the answer to this should be positive. However, this should not be assumed. A final review session must be conducted. Preferably, a provisional date for this will be fixed well in advance to alert essential attendees to reserve the time. The meeting should include representatives from the team, the work process and executive management. Apart from analysing whether the original objective has been met, attention needs to focus on performance improvement at the benchmark partner's process as well as any other external evidence of process supremos. Depending on the length of time taken for the benchmarking exercise, others will possibly have improved also. As seen in Step 8, the world does not stop revolving while one man benchmarks!

Some guidelines for the Step 12 review are suggested below.

- ☐ Fix a provisional review date at the outset when objectives are agreed and commitment is high.
- ☐ Confirm this as soon as is reasonable; if left too near the end of the exercise the danger is that people will be too busy fighting the next battle.
- ☐ In addition to your process, ensure that evidence is available of external practices other than just the benchmark.
- ☐ Consider the following questions:

  - ○ Have the objectives been met?
  - ○ What is the evidence of improvement?
  - ○ How high is commitment?
  - ○ If high, is it sustainable?
  - ○ Was the exercise efficient and effective?

- ☐ What needs to be done to improve benchmarking skills before the next benchmarking exercise?
- ☐ Is there a need for (more) training?
- ☐ Is our process now where we want it to be?
- ☐ Can it be placed on the low-burner and attention turned elsewhere? Or is further work required?
- ☐ Who is the on-going process champion?
- ☐ What mechanism is in place to maintain the improvement/signal the need for further improvement in the future?
- ☐ How effective have communications been?
- ☐ Have benchmarking approaches in respect of this process been received from other organisations?
- ☐ How can we become still more outward looking?
- ☐ When should this process be reviewed again?

The review session should supply evidence and information on which to base decisions about future courses of action. There may be instances during the introductory phase of benchmarking when it is necessary to recycle the whole exercise because objectives have not been met. This will more usually become apparent during, rather than at the end of, the 12-step process.

When benchmarking is integrated into the culture, the final review will provide evidence of the results of desired improvements on business performance. The key factor then is to build regular formal review in to the on-going management procedures to avoid possible regression. Depending on the level of the process, a suitable opportunity might be afforded during annual performance assessment/objective setting with the process owner or at the senior executive business strategy planning session.

Chapter Ten

Maintaining leadership

Internal audit marks progress

New information adds dynamism

Executive in charge of business reviews

THE NEED for change and improvement, if not welcomed, is at least justifiable when the competitive climate is grim and the economic cycle at its lowest point. However, those companies riding the crest of a wave with booming profits, could be forgiven for putting change near the bottom of the list of priorities.

'We're doing OK as we are, so don't rock the boat!' is a familiar phrase. But complacency can lead to downfall, as the Swiss discovered.

For example, geography has played a major role in Switzerland's industrial development. The high proportion of land unsuitable for cultivation has, over the centuries, led to an economy more reliant on trade and industry than agriculture. Moreover, widely dispersed settlements encouraged livelihoods dependent on crafts and skills handed down through generations.

Legendary among these was, of course, watch and clock making. Based in the Jura towns around Geneva, this industry had, by the 19th century, given the Swiss a global monopoly. Swiss watches were synonymous with excellence until well into the mid 20th century.

By the second half of this century, however, a member of the Swiss watchmaking fraternity was experimenting with non-traditional 'movements'. Eventually he devised a working model with no jewels or mainspring and yet was an accurate timepiece. With pride he presented his revolutionary new technology at the annual Horologists Convention where he expected it to meet with enthusiasm and wonder.

Instead the reaction was shock and incomprehension. How could *anyone*, and a Swiss at that, call something with no jewels, levers or complex movements, a Watch? The idea was dismissed with perfunctory civility. By the Swiss.

Yet several years later Seiko took the world by storm and almost overnight demolished the Swiss monopoly. Today it is impossible to imagine a world without the quartz watch.

Success, as this example shows, breeds within it the seeds of its own destruction. Time and again, a single good idea revolutionises years of tradition and practice. Of course, if that idea is your country's or company's then you are laughing. If not ...

Just 10 years ago, Tom Peters and Bob Waterman published their landmark book which probably did more to spark the current quality/customer debate than any other. Since then 'In Search of Excellence' has become almost better known as a record of 'Those were the great that were'. Which conveys no disrespect of the companies which have subsequently run into doldrums. Their fate could be anybody's.

Having climbed the ladder to excellence, or, as in the case with benchmarking, the 12 steps to be World Best, how can companies avoid the seemingly inevitable slippery slide down into the abyss on the other side?

Excellent management of the business and its resources is obviously essential; a number of estimable texts published over the past five years give clues to achieving this. Additional impetus is provided by the continuous review and improvement ethos that is built into benchmarking.

As an increasing number of processes come under the benchmarking microscope, ever more people are trained in the philosophy of review as an integral part of continuous improvement. Hence, over time it becomes second nature to a growing percentage of the organisation's population. Unfortunately, relying on this notion alone to maintain best performance in what inevitably will be a progressively fierce competitive arena is insufficient.

Re-calibrating the company

Formal reviews of processes which have attained benchmark status should be carried out at annual intervals, most logically as part of the business planning cycle. Often referred to as 're-calibration' this centres on: reviewing the measurements of benchmarked processes to ensure they are still valid in the light of any external changes, and reassessing the penetration of the benchmarking philosophy throughout the organisation.

As with all benchmarking activities, the most effective method is to start with an internal audit. This is followed by revisiting the best practice partner to establish how far it has progressed. (Gathering information from other than the partner company is part of a broader on-going 'excellence' review).

The internal audit should gauge the extent to which gaps exist in the benchmark information, their nature and scope, (these could be new gaps which have been revealed during the exercise, or originals, never satisfactorily closed - maybe due to cultural or other exigencies or because they were not considered critical); and whether, and by how much, attitudes towards and understanding of benchmarking have changed since the exercise was completed or last reviewed.

Having detailed and up-to-date knowledge in these internal areas gives greater purpose to the external aspects of the review. It will be necessary in most cases to carry out some kind of employee attitude survey to ascertain this knowledge. This may vary in scope from all-embracing, formal questionnaires to informal face-to-face sample interviews, or inclusion as a small part of another survey. Much will depend on the culture of the organisation, and the 'age' of the benchmarking programme.

Seeking new or challenging information adds a dynamic dimension to checking previously gathered and recorded data. The experience and benefit of hindsight play a vital role in the re-calibration process. Even if the data and information are the same, they may be subject to different interpretations after, as opposed to before, the integration of benchmarking.

Additionally, feedback from the attitude survey will help keep the direction and focus of the company's benchmarking approach in tune with the perceptions and development of its people and with their acceptance and understanding of the new philosophy. It will highlight areas of weakness or misdirection, indicating where greater emphasis is needed. This in turn helps in the allocation of resources to those areas where the most impact will be felt.

INTERNAL AUDIT: THE ACCEPTANCE OF BENCHMARKING

When undertaking an internal audit, consideration of the following should be included:

- [ ] How important is benchmarking in strategy planning?
- [ ] How far is this reflected in annual business planning?
- [ ] How far is it incorporated into individual objectives?
- [ ] What value is benchmarking perceived to have added to business and resource management?
- [ ] Is the systematic process understood?
- [ ] How much training is being given in the technique?
- [ ] How much up-dating training is being given on a needs basis?
- [ ] In which areas is learning most required?
- [ ] How are acceptance, understanding and value of benchmarking measured?
- [ ] How much have they increased since the previous review?
- [ ] What improvements are being made to the benchmarking process?

So far two aspects of review have been covered:

☐ As the twelfth step in each benchmarking exercise; and
☐ As an on-going iterative component of the process and progress of benchmarking within the company.

To complete the review in terms of maintaining leadership a third aspect must be considered:

☐ The panoramic overview or reconnaissance of worldwide best practices.

This is quite distinct from the every-day running of the business. The responsibility for this should be carried by someone well equipped to identify, interpret and translate best practices in the context of their impact on the mission and vision of the company. Such an individual will probably, but not necessarily, be a member of the senior executive team.

The business review executive

This can be assisted by the appointment of a business review executive (BRE). This person has expert knowledge of the company's processes and systems; access to a well constructed global network of leading edge thinkers in academia, marketing, science and technology; and a restless creative mind with boundless energy and enthusiasm for positive change and continuous improvement. Contrary to the rumbustious image this may conjure up, the suitable personality is as likely to be a self-reliant quiet thinker and listener with detailed understanding of the corporate architecture.

The person selected for this role would be expected to:

- [ ] Have expert knowledge of company processes and systems
- [ ] Have a thorough grasp of the corporate architecture
- [ ] Have access to a global network of leading edge thinkers in business and academia
- [ ] Have positive energy and enthusiasm for change
- [ ] Constantly question the status quo, challenging perceptions and exploding paradigms
- [ ] Have an enquiring mind, coupled with energy and enthusiasm
- [ ] Be proactive and externally focused
- [ ] Be a creative, lateral but practical thinker
- [ ] Become the corporation bee, constantly cross-fertilising internal ideas and best practices with those seen and heard outside the organisation

And finally, since the change agent is not inured to the impact of change:

- [ ] The individual should fulfil this role for a maximum of three years.

Up to three-quarters of the BRE's remit - to be the global eyes and ears of the company - is conducted away from the office. Through a distillation of leading edge thinking, writing and practice, the executive is responsible for feeding back into the organisation that which may enhance its performance.

The balance of the remit is conducted back at base. Liaising at all levels, roaming, questioning, examining and probing into activities and processes, the role of the BRE is designed to constantly challenge perceptions and explode the organisation's paradigms. A supreme devil's advocate! The purpose is to nip complacency in the bud before it has the chance to mature and become dangerous.

Some companies already have such an 'agent provocateur' in place. The role encompasses the additional traits needed to keep the organisation on its toes and provide it with the highest probability of 'seeing' from where opportunities and threats are likely to come.

Chapter Eleven

Case histories of benchmarking in practice

THERE IS much to be learned from other firms' experiences. This chapter presents six companies which have introduced benchmarking in Europe and adopted it as one of their strategic management tools.

The cases are drawn from manufacturing industry, the service sector, and 'Third Wave' information technology companies. They include elements of internal, external and best practice benchmarking.

They are not intended as Harvard-type studies but rather as role models. They describe some of the lessons learned, hurdles overcome, and progress achieved.

Fig 11.1 Companies which have adopted benchmarking

Sector	Company	Benchmarking		
		Internal	External	Best practice
Traditional Manufacturing	1. Shell Chemicals UK			
	2. Hawker Fusegear			
	3. Rover Group			
Service Sector	4. TNT Express			
Third Wave	5. Digital Equipment			
	6. Hewlett Packard			

1. Shell Chemicals UK Ltd

*PREVIOUS chapters have shown how benchmarking efforts
are aided considerably when there is supportive leadership of,
and commitment to, continuous improvement from the top of
the organisation. If to this is added focus on the external
environment, openness to new ideas and a willingness to
incorporate benchmarking into corporate strategy, then the
commitment of business and line management will more
readily follow.*

This has been the experience at Shell Chemicals UK Ltd
(SCUK), one of the major divisions within Shell
Transport & Trading, the UK's third largest company by
market capitalisation. It is also part of the Royal Dutch/
Shell Group which employs a total of 135,000 people
worldwide.

In the latter part of 1990 the senior management team at
SCUK were assessing a number of techniques that could
enhance the company's Total Quality Management
programme. Following considerable research and
discussion it was agreed that benchmarking could
provide the rational structure that would help businesses
gain optimum improvement and, hence, returns. The
responsibility for benchmarking was devolved to the
business managers at the end of that year and during
1991 some 14 benchmarking teams were brought
together to analyse and define the company's critical
success factors which, in turn, would identify the key
processes to which benchmarking could be applied.

Valuable learning points arose even in the early stages.
There was undoubted commitment to the technique and

the teams met frequently to identify the areas of value to examine. Despite the considerable energy and effort invested, however, the first few months proved difficult with little visible progress being made.

Analysis of the underlying problem suggested there was insufficient understanding of *'how to'* benchmark. Original critical success factors proved too large and unfocused and their definition nebulous; consequently they were difficult to measure. The solution was to develop suitable training for the benchmarking teams.

Rather than reinvent the wheel, SCUK looked for and identified organisations which had successfully implemented benchmarking programmes. Discussing their experiences and 'picking brains' led to a prototype design which was then moulded to suit the company's needs and culture. By the middle of the year workshops were in place to provide the skills the teams required to manage the process.

Throughout 1991 the teams worked to identify, define and analyse their critical business success factors in the light of what had been learned from their workshops. They describe progress during this period as analogous to advancing through quicksand - a slow, constant struggle to get anywhere. During this 'struggle', however, they learned what others before, and since, have also realised. Whilst the areas selected for benchmarking were deemed to be most useful they had not necessarily been accurately, or correctly, defined. The challenge was to find the master key to each process, acknowledging that the first example found was not always the right one. In other words, they had to keep asking: 'Hey! What do we actually mean by that?' This is *the* recurring phrase throughout benchmarking. A business process is like an onion; each layer peeled off reveals yet another layer, and another .....

The constant necessity to analyse, define and reanalyse operational processes has proved educational in itself and of great value to the company. Within a year of setting up the benchmarking programme the teams have reintroduced basic flow chart methodology to break processes down to their *smallest* part to allow the critical factors to be defined and measured accurately. The original 'sequential step' model, which provided the foundation for the training, has also evolved into a more fluid version. It now allows for the fact that, in practice, the 'steps' may be completed contemporaneously or out of sequence. This does not affect the thoroughness with which each step is completed but may result in shorter cycle times for the benchmarking process.

Other lessons learned are reflected in the following specific example of benchmarking in the business.

One critical area identified at the outset of 1991 was continuity of supply. More specifically, moving some 700k tonnes of feedstocks to chemical plants throughout the UK. Limited logistics and storage necessitate detailed planning of this operation. Discontinuity of supply can result in plants having to shut-down; this is costly and fraught with knock-on problems.

The objective of the benchmarking study was to improve contingency planning. The management team brought together a cross-functional group of eight, drawn from marketing, distribution, movements, finance and pipeline operations. The first team meeting held in January 1991 was followed up with regular sessions to brainstorm critical success factors, conduct flowchart analyses and identify data required and potential benchmark partners. This work resulted in two companies being selected as suitable contacts.

Planning process data were gathered internally and followed through by contacting the selected companies. Letters sent to key people were followed up over the telephone. The external contacts were keen, in principle, to arrange meetings to discuss the potential gains but were insufficiently aware of the benchmarking technique, or not so far down the Total Quality route, to understand how it could benefit both parties. SCUK quickly realised that, in addition to developing acceptance of the new philosophy and concept internally, they had to develop similar acceptance in their benchmark companies before work could begin. After many weeks of 'education', discussion and negotiation, however, agreement was reached with the two organisations to share information.

One of these has proved to be very fruitful. Performance gaps, linked to quantitative measurements, have been identified by detailed analysis and process comparison.

Where it is of interest to the benchmark partner, the information is freely shared. The co-operative dialogue is keen since the 'partner' subsequently identified one of its key processes at which it recognises SCUK to be 'best'. This has therefore become the subject of a second benchmarking exercise between the two companies.

Both sides of this partnership have discovered the similarities in culture and management style that have assisted their efforts. This is an unexpected bonus. Superior performance can owe as much to management behaviour and attitude as to measurably better processes. No matter how willing companies are to benchmark against each other, efforts can be frustrated, or even abandoned, if the culture and operational climate are found to be too dissimilar.

It is too early to know what operational changes may result from the detailed work involved. Sufficient progress has been made, however, to convince SCUK that it will continue down this route and that benchmarking will be one of the quality tools with which it will work to improve performance in key operations. Difficulties encountered (such as those resulting from unfocused targets or defining too wide an output to measure successfully), and the lessons learned, are regularly communicated to other Product Business Teams through seminars. This is resulting in a clearer understanding of the business and operational processes, as well as of the technique itself, spreading through the organisation.

Senior managers at Shell Chemicals UK Ltd recognise that no one person or organisation can have a monopoly on all the good ideas. There is much to be learned from establishing good relationships in non-competitive areas. Viewed in this light they see no limitations to gradually adopting benchmarking in most corporate activities and have no hesitation in recommending its use to others.

Whilst acknowledging that returns will not be apparent overnight the benchmarking teams now feel that, instead of struggling through quicksand, their path is leading along a fairly firm beach with only occasional flurries of sand blowing in their eyes!

2. Hawker Fusegear Ltd

BENCHMARKING is one of the latest additions to the Total Quality Management tool kit. It is not surprising, therefore, that many benchmarking endeavours are spawned within an organisation's Quality Department. This has been the experience of Hawker Fusegear Ltd, part of the Hawker Siddeley Group which, following a takeover during 1991, is now part of the BTR conglomerate.

Hawker Fusegear began in Lambeth in 1879 when a pioneering Victorian, Charles Francis Brush, set up a factory to manufacture brush fuses for London's power stations. Ten years later he bought the Falcon Engineering & Car Company at Loughborough, Leicestershire, and relocated the Brush Factory to that county where it has remained since. In 1890 Charles Brush lodged the first patent for HRC fuses providing arc-quenching material which revolutionised the industry and led to the development of electric lighting along the Embankment.

The company continued to lead innovation in its field, growing from strength to strength until, in 1957, it became part of the Hawker Siddeley Group. As a mark of its reputation, it retained its original name and continued to make fuses in most parts of the Brush Group. Eventually, however, the importance of this activity led to reorganisation and after 26 years fuse manufacture was brought together in one part of the group and renamed Brush Fusegear. In 1987 it was overtly brought under the Hawker Siddeley banner and restyled 'Hawker Fusegear'.

Based at the former RAF bomber training site at Wymeswold the company employs 272 people and manufactures a range of fuses from the smallest instrument-protection fuses (just slightly larger than the domestic kind) to the largest 1m fuses used in power generation.

Within its nine-strong quality section it has a quality manager who is a pioneer of the new world. Impressed by the benefits of benchmarking as soon as he read of the technique in 1989, he set out to demonstrate that what could be achieved within a large multinational organisation could improve also the processes within a relatively small specialised company.

Identifying contract review within the commercial department as a critical success factor, he set about benchmarking with the objective of reducing errors at order intake.

Although at a later stage a small cross-functional group of people was brought together as a team to progress improvements, the quality manager conducted much of the early work himself. The process he identified consisted of taking orders by telephone, letter or facsimile and placing them into a computerised system. Having isolated the elements within this process, he then set out to find a benchmark partner with a system giving minimum or zero errors.

Realising one was unlikely to be found in his firm's specialised sector, the quality manager organised a brainstorming session. This led to informal visits to Argos Showrooms - selected because of its speed of response to orders. Whilst this threw up some interesting ideas, most elements in the process were too dissimilar to emulate. It was while at a British Quality Association meeting that a chance conversation with a senior manager from Butterley Brick Ltd led to a co-operative benchmarking exercise. The objective now was to understand the process which led to Butterley Brick being able to maintain zero errors at contract review and nil duplication of orders.

Field visits were set up between the two companies to view and map the office processes and determine the essential differences and gaps. Eventually, Butterley Brick's Nottingham office system was adapted and introduced at the Fusegear site.

Whilst mapping out the process it was found that a combination of history and habit at Fusegear had created an interesting disfunction - the sales staff had developed the habit of pre-stamping orders, on the assumption that they would automatically be completed. Anyone trying to establish the status of an order beyond that point could, therefore, mistakenly assume that it was completed and no further action would ensue. This resulted in incomplete orders, customer complaints and duplications arising from attempts to rectify errors.

The introduction of a relatively straightforward step - using stamps *only* to sign off orders when actually complete - dramatically decreased errors and eliminated duplications.

Progress was monitored and the number of customer complaints received used to quantify the success rate. At the same time, previously unremarked non-compliances on internal audit against the quality manual came to light. Again, the remedy was quite straightforward; the manual was updated to reflect the new internal audit system.

At each stage, when a gap was found and the anomalies identified, corrective action was audited by the quality manager. By early 1991 the target of zero errors had been achieved. Throughout this process the quality manager has maintained a dialogue and shared information with Butterley Brick. Likewise, successes achieved have been communicated throughout the company.

In many companies benchmarking has been successfully implemented because of top-level commitment and a corporate goal based on improvement through benchmarking. In the case of Hawker Fusegear, however, it is personal commitment and enthusiasm, coupled with faith in a new approach, which has driven the process forward. Having achieved the first goal and the commitment of a cross-functional team, a second area for improvement - storage - has been identified and a benchmarking exercise is being planned.

There are other areas within the company which will receive similar attention in their turn, thus ensuring that benchmarking will remain ongoing and become integrated within the company's planning for continuous improvement.

3. Rover Body & Pressings

ONE of the basic prerequisites for benchmarking is the will to improve and to become the 'best of the best'. It is enshrined in Japanese culture where it translates as 'Dantotsu', incorporating the essence of the process used to gain competitive advantage. It is not surprising, therefore, to find a British company with the will to be 'best' optimising its collaborative relationship with a Japanese company to produce a practical benchmarking programme.

In early 1990 Rover Group initiated a benchmarking programme, choosing the Body & Pressings division to pilot this within the group. Using a simple process, developed from the Xerox approach, their objective was to use benchmarking as part of the Total Quality Management tool kit to promote operational process ownership and improvement throughout the organisation.

Attempts to benchmark can rapidly flounder if another principle is not realised. That is, the key processes which govern business outputs, not the outputs themselves must be the focus of benchmarking efforts. Anyone who thinks it is a rapid panacea to alleviate poor returns is sadly disillusioned.

The programme initiated in Rover's Body & Pressings division is grounded on this principle. It is 'How' things are done which is important. This reinforces the importance of processes. No amount of looking at best practice will help unless there is a full understanding of how the processes work.

Rover Body & Pressings has identified two distinct process levels. The first level incorporates the basic processes of the business unit; for example, pre-manufacturing logistics and manufacturing itself. These are then unbundled to disclose the second level processes which, in the case of manufacture, for example, include tool changeover, panel pressing and machine maintenance. At each level a process owner is identified and made responsible for making it happen. Each first and second level process is thoroughly analysed to identify the elements within them, such as lead time or stock accuracy; these must be measured to ensure achievement of the critical success factors.

What Hewlett Packard has called the Onion Factor - peeling away one process layer to reveal another, and another, and yet another - Rover has termed the 'Virtuous Circle'. The analysis adopted at the first and second level processes can be applied progressively throughout the organisation and as it permeates through each activity the whole business can become geared towards improvement. Moreover, the teams undertaking the improvement actions can relate their contribution to the achievement of overall business targets.

Benchmarking visits are arranged only when the Rover teams have completed their analyses and are thoroughly familiar with their processes. This 'preparation' before a visit ensures they fully appreciate and can use the knowledge gained from the world class operation being studied.

As an example of this Rover executives cite the number of times staff from the Body & Pressings division visited Honda plants in the pre-benchmarking era. One performance aspect noted particularly was that Honda changeover times were more than 10 times quicker. At the time this was dismissed on the basis that such speed could not be applied to Rover's own seemingly older machines. Recently, however, a team was established to focus specifically on press line performance and changeover times. After two months of improvement actions the team visited Honda plants in Japan where members were surprised to see that in many cases the Japanese equipment was no better than their own. The performance difference was due to the degree of attention to detail. It was not what machinery was being used but *how* which enabled Honda to achieve such high performance levels.

Over 2,000 implementable improvement ideas resulted from the visit to which were coupled a positive mental attitude that helps the teams achieve what otherwise they had thought impossible.

Whilst the benchmarking teams are making significant progress they would acknowledge that even with all the will in the world they could not have achieved this without the absolute commitment of the senior management team. They correctly identify this as being as critical to benchmarking as process orientation. The Quality Council, a Rover Group board team, the aim of which is to improve Total Quality within the entire Rover Group, actively benchmarks its own activities as well as the Quality Council process to establish further opportunities for improvement.

To this commitment is coupled a strong vision and strategic direction for the business, providing a firm framework for all benchmarking activities. The management understands the orientation and focus of the business and within this can gear improvements to key critical success factors.

This combination of process orientation and ownership, total commitment from the top and strong vision adds up to an extremely powerful catalyst for change. It sets an example which other would-be benchmarkers would do well to consider.

4. TNT Express (UK) Ltd

BENCHMARKING is often perceived as a management tool for use only in diverse, multinational groups. Much of this perception is due to its origins in Xerox Corporation in the US and subsequent adoption by other large concerns, such as General Electric and AT&T. In fact, there is every reason why smaller organisations should find it less, not more, difficult to integrate into their management processes than such vast corporations. They may, for example, be less bureaucratic, more open to 'new' ideas, more entrepreneurial in their response to market trends and needs, and have fewer faint hearts to win over internally.

One UK group which has integrated benchmarking into its culture and practice is TNT Express (UK) Ltd based at Atherstone in Warwickshire. Alan Jones, chief executive of TNT Express (UK) Ltd describes the group's business as Third Party Contracting but it could more appositely be called 'Customer Solutions'.

What this means in practice was exemplified during the fundamental reorganisation of the newspaper industry, which culminated in, and was subsequently referred to colloquially as, the 'Wapping crisis'. TNT Newsfast had just five hours' notice to implement its plan to take over all of Rupert Murdoch's News International newspaper transport business, which entails the movement of around 5,000 tonnes of newsprint each week. Although operational systems were planned and ready to implement, the controversy over the print unions meant that no-one knew the start date or, indeed, if the 'job' would ever go ahead. The go-ahead was finally given late on a Friday evening. All management staff worked overtime throughout the weekend, recruiting staff to enable the new contract to be covered without detracting from service to the company's regular customers. By Monday morning the 1,000 extra people needed to operate the newspaper contract had been recruited.

Listening to customer needs and problems has led to such innovations as double-decker HGV trailers; roller cages which reduce unloading time for a 40ft trailer to 2min; hydraulic cranes which can shift forward after the trailer is unloaded at a building site to help provide the traction to propel the vehicle out of even the most cloying quagmire; and improved aerodynamics which reduce the coefficient drag on a standard HGV from 0.75 to 0.41 to give a saving in fuel costs of 12-20% (depending on the weight of the driver's boots). These are only a few representative examples.

In addition to this impressive innovation record, TNT Express (UK) Ltd was the 1991 Motor Transport Industry Customer Care Award winner and the first (and so far only) transport company to achieve BS5750 Parts I and II. Over an 18 month period to April 1992, the company managed to cut the unit cost in one of its businesses by 14% and throughout 1991 added to its list of trading customers by 12%.

Benchmarking is just one of the tools it has used to achieve an eminent presence among the 30 or so of its fierce competitors which make up the UK contract transport and express delivery market.

Unlike many large organisations which turn to benchmarking as a route through, or solution to, crisis conditions, TNT has 'grown' its approach over the past decade. It now comprises four well-trodden steps:

- [ ] Analysis and understanding of processes;
- [ ] Establishing present position by identifying and comparing with 'world class' players and areas of excellence;
- [ ] Formulating and implementing action plans; and
- [ ] Continuously assessing and improving.

When it first started trading in 1978 the senior managers knew that entry barriers to their chosen field were not easy to overcome. They decided from the outset that their only route lay in being the best in every sector of the transport market in which they chose to operate. To succeed and become profitable they analysed all the processes which made up costs and eliminated those which did not add value. This was combined with minute attention to detail, 'removal' of the potential for error from the start and a culture centred on solving customer problems.

Supporting this was, and is, a common-sense approach to harnessing every employee's brainpower; a philosophy of keeping all systems as simple as possible; praise, reward and recognition for all ideas generated; open-door management; use of first names throughout the company; a promotion-by-merit environment and a reward system in which all employees are on output-related bonus. This has engendered a 'make it happen' (instead of 'can do') atmosphere in which everyone rolls up their sleeves and works to make their company the best there is. Incidentally, this is the company which provides Rover Group staff with 'the last 10 minutes of the movie' (see p119).

As a third party contractor, TNT is working for numerous clients in a wide variety of industries. As a result, the company is able to develop standards of best practice for every aspect of its operations through the experience gained within its core business. TNT UK has also benchmarked its operations against similar activities performed within the TNT Groups in other parts of the world.

Each benchmarking exercise is based on an analysis of the processes and begins with a blank sheet of paper. There are no pre-conceived ideas; instead of asking 'How is this done', team members question 'How could this best be done'. To establish the present position the benchmarking team identifies world class players, examining areas of excellence and detailing comparisons. All relevant information is analysed to establish best methods of operation, process times and unit costs. Lessons learned are then applied to TNT's practices. In this way it has, for example, developed what it believes is the best and most efficient warehouse 'picking' process.

When analysis is complete, the strategy is established and resources allocated. Then the implementation plan and timescales are formulated. Targets are clear, achievable and realistic. This is not to suggest they are necessarily comfortable. The emphasis is on demanding effort and stretching individuals' abilities in order to instil a sense of achievement and pride, as well as the highest of standards.

Once a process has become the benchmark it is regularly reassessed at special review meetings. Keeping abreast of innovation and new technologies is integral to this. Where possible these are incorporated in existing processes; these are never cast in stone but are constantly subject to up-dating and improvement.

TNT applies benchmarking in every area of its business to make sure each is of the best. Its experience is shared with the customers so that they receive the best service from TNT and have the opportunity of benchmarking themselves, initially against TNT, to become the best in their own field.

The information, knowledge and expertise gathered through this constant benchmarking cycle is one factor which supports TNT's insistence that it can never rest on its laurels. It will continue to use benchmarking for the powerful tool it has become and to help its customers achieve greater profitability. TNT's one exclusion clause is that it will never consider benchmarking against or with any of its direct competitors in the UK.

5. Digital Equipment Corporation (DEC)

DURING the late 1980s the computer industry, like many others, was facing up to an increasingy harsh environment. The industry itself was also changing as growth slowed and margins shrank. In 1989 Digital Equipment Corporation (DEC) carried out a strategic review at the company's headquarters in the US. This concluded that financial efficiency would become increasingly critical to the success of the business. The corollary to this was to focus on overheads and find areas where significant savings could be made.

A team was chartered to look at work and organisation redesign. Its remit was to study the corporation from the outside in, to discover areas where DEC was perceived by outsiders to be best in class and others which offered opportunities for improvement.

Using a benchmarking process adapted from the Xerox model, the team identified companies and work categories, devised questions and visited recognised best in class companies such as IBM, Canon, Motorola, Sony, Ricoh and Ford. The justification for looking at a preponderance of Japanese companies was 'that was where the toughest competition emanated from'. In each case the team studied financial processes from the organisation (work) and cultural perspective. Comparing these with their own processes highlighted potential sources of savings in areas including information systems and access, organisation and role structure as well as the financial processes themselves.

Analysing the findings led to a choice of three possible scenarios:

A. significant improvement/greatest upheaval;

B. considerable improvement/considerable upheaval, and

C. acceptable improvement/minimum upheaval.

The goal of a 25% reduction in cost within three years, one outcome of the middle course of action, was confirmed finally as the most reasonable way forward. Scenario A was rejected chiefly because of the reduction in staff numbers which it required.

In order to achieve its goal DEC adopted Total Quality Management (TQM) as the corporate-wide term for a set of four inter-related initiatives - 'The voice of the customer'; 'six sigma performance'; 'cycle time reduction' and 'benchmarking'. All were aimed at achieving higher levels of customer satisfaction and providing competitive costs in all activities. The congruent initiatives rested on voluntary employee involvement, which in turn demanded leadership commitment and a considerable investment in employee education.

Each of these attributes is exemplified in the payroll department, where the manager is firmly committed to TQM through training individuals to work smarter not harder. The business has become the internal benchmark for DEC and has recently been rated Best in Class (from a short list of 15 US and six Japanese companies) by a major firm of consultants. The operation comprises just 26 people. It pays 60,000 employees at 320 locations, 14% of them with individual cheques, on a weekly basis. The manager knows the job plan for each of his staff; moreover, each plan is visible to all members of the group. Additionally, each individual is empowered to modify his or her own plan whenever conditions change.

Every department member receives 10 days training a year in total quality related techniques in order to help meet their personal objectives within the context of the department's three customer oriented goals. Furthermore, every employee has a copy of the long range plan, a 30-page professional brochure, so they have the opportunity to understand how their role contributes to attaining these goals.

DEC regards building co-reliance and combining continuous improvement efforts as a journey, rather than an event, the outcome of which will allow it to become a better listener and more willing learner in its selective drive to set new benchmarks. DEC stresses that it is vital for the focus of any benchmarking exercise to be both well chosen and grounded within the whole organisation. This means a commitment to hard work and discipline.

Other lessons learned include the need for a framework for all benchmarking activity; allowing more time than is available; keeping objectives constantly in mind; developing actionable follow-through and, most crucial, having a dedicated sponsor.

The framework which the company has evolved comprises four steps;

1. What to benchmark?
2. How is it done here?
3. Who is best?
    and
4. How do they do it?

Only those factors which significantly affect the overall competitive position of the company are selected for benchmarking.

Throughout its activities, DEC stresses the importance of the systematic approach. This means ensuring correct understanding prevails from the outset. Positioning it in a proper context is a prerequisite before even thinking about taking the first step. Misuse, suggests UK quality manager, Mike Newell, arises from 'advocacies without enquiry'. That is:

☐   'We must reduce our costs by 25%' (to equal the benchmark figure).
     (Consequence: cost reduction can lead to value decrease for customers.)

Or

☐   'We need to let X (the benchmark) people go'.
     (Consequence: symptoms are tackled without understanding the cause of the difference.)

No-one has prescient knowledge of what will ultimately decide which companies become, and endure as, best in class. DEC, however, lists three messages which could be top of the list for all aspiring organisations:

- ☐ Identify with a critical success factor that is customer focused;
- ☐ Get to know the related process capabilities really well; and
- ☐ Benchmark in the context of experiential and action oriented learning.

A customer-oriented organisation cannot escape the long-term consequences of poor performance. Hence, DEC believes, the real success factors are linked with customer values which in turn throws the spotlight on key areas where things must go right if the business is to prosper and flourish.

6. Hewlett Packard Ltd

A KEY FEATURE of benchmarking, whether internal, external or best practice, is its focus on processes as opposed to outputs. Rigorous analysis and understanding of internal processes, which frequently leads to significant performance improvement, also provide benchmarking teams with the foundation for their visits to 'best practice' sites. Hewlett Packard is one company which has adopted process analysis as an essential part of its Total Quality Culture and then used it to drive its benchmarking programme.

Hewlett Packard was first established in the UK in Bedford in 1961. Since then its has grown to four divisions employing a total of 4,100 people, with a head office in Bracknell, Berkshire. This is the largest operation, employing 2,100; it is also the UK sales region office. Its operations include the Queensferry Terminal divisions based on the outskirts of Edinburgh. Other sites include Bristol for computer peripherals and a research and development Office Products division based at Crowthorne, Berkshire.

Understanding where Hewlett Packard is today and how benchmarking has helped its journey to Total Quality, requires a step back to the mid-1970s. At that time, one of its sister divisions, Yokogawa Hewlett Packard, based in Japan, had to compete against up-and-coming players in its home market. Its performance in most key areas was worse then than that of many of Hewlett Packard's other worldwide entities.

Yokogawa Hewlett Packard realised that bold goals were essential if the company was to stay competitive. In 1976 the division set itself the objective of winning the coveted Deming Prize by 1983 - a seven-year goal. To achieve this, it set out to improve its performance in every aspect of the business. The search for ways to do this led management to analyse everything they did and treat each step forward, no matter how big or small, with equal respect.

Not only did they reach their goal, but they did so a year earlier than planned - in 1982. This then set the precedent that Hewlett Packard worldwide would follow, clearly setting the company on the road to Total Quality control.

The philosophy of continuous improvement is now ingrained into every aspect of the company's operations. Despite, or perhaps because of this, it realises that businesses it is not even aware of are also improving constantly. It has realised that continuous improvement cannot proceed in isolation; it needs to be aware of what is happening outside the company to ensure that its improvements really keep pace with that of others.

The company's UK sales region constantly use best practice benchmarking to monitor and assess practices and processes existing outside its operation. In this it sets an example in the technique for many of its European partner operations.

Internal benchmarking against other Hewlett Packard divisions and entities by the UK sales region is ongoing. This is not confined to a study of UK operations, but encompasses visits in Europe, North American, Japan and Singapore. These 'internal' visits have proved a useful learning experience in how to set about benchmarking and many of the lessons learned have been applied to the often more challenging external benchmarking visits.

Hewlett Packard stresses the importance of identifying the process that is to be the subject of the benchmarking study. Although this sounds a relatively simple task, in practice managers have found it one of the most challenging aspects of any benchmark programme. Of great help has been the company's ongoing initiative on process management; this has resulted in the identification of a wide range of key processes and process owners.

Hewlett Packard's UK sales region has seen many improvement opportunities whilst undertaking external best practice benchmarking. Key areas of the business, such as order fulfilment, credit collection and sales finance have come under the microscope. In many cases this involved multiple visits to a number of different partners.

In all cases the teams sought to identify fully and understand their own processes before studying those of others. They found this considerably enhanced the effectiveness of the visits and resulted in the collection of large amounts of useful information. The common key to the teams' successes has been the fact that they all communicated their findings extensively and networked comprehensively, resulting in effective sharing of best practices.

Whilst on visits, the teams concentrated on analysing the 'soft' narrative behind the 'hard' performance metrics. Thus, a much deeper understanding of their partner's practices was gained: importantly, they attempted to ascertain the intangible reasons behind the exemplary performance.

A measure of Hewlett Packard's success in its benchmarking programmes is the increasing number of visits they *receive* from other organisations benchmarking *them*. Benchmarking is becoming part of the culture within the company; programmes, rather than being driven from the centre, often begin when individuals enthusiastically set them up themselves to tackle specific issues in their business areas.

Best practice benchmarking will remain ongoing at Hewlett Packard. The company recognises the competitive market place is dynamic and ever changing. New nations and companies are constantly leaping to the forefront at the leading edge of industry. For Hewlett Packard, benchmarking is a means by which it can ensure that it is always aware of, and striving to adopt, best practices wherever they are occurring.

Chapter Twelve

Managing benchmarking in the organisation

Balancing the interests of the business . . .

With those of the customer

Four phases to development

BENCHMARKING is one of a number of initiatives or tools that can be employed by companies undergoing a change strategy. As seen in Chapter Three, benchmarking will most usually link in to the Quality Improvement and Problem Solving processes. Depending on the degree and level of change required these may include other initiatives such as Just-in-Time (JIT), Simultaneous Engineering, Statistical Process Control (SPC), Electronic Data Interchange (EDI), Total Productive Maintenance (TPM), Total Cost Reduction (TCR), and so on.

Whether benchmarking is the prime change motivator, or is secondary to another initiative, it must be managed to ensure optimum effectiveness of both the process and its contribution to other management processes of the business - the planning and budgetary cycles, for example.

In progressing towards becoming 'best of the best' in what is produced and in the processes and resources employed in providing excellence, companies will become more efficient in the use of (always scarce) resources. This may involve freeing up people, or capacity and/or producing more of what the customer wants.

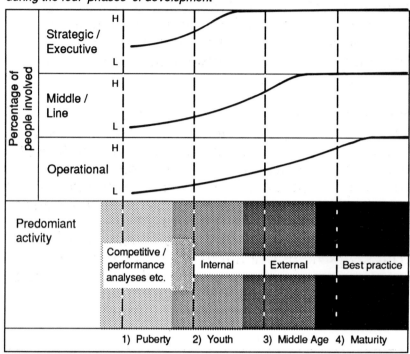

Fig 12.1 Predominant benchmarking activity and management involvement during the four 'phases' of development

Notes: 1. Competitive / performance analyses frequently precede formal benchmarking either as a separate activity or as a means of establishing the company's relative standing prior to launching formal benchmarking.

2. The predominant activity will generally 'straddle' the transition from one 'age' to the next.

3. As benchmarking reaches late maturity many, if not all, these activities are likely to be going on at the same time.

Management must balance the interests of the company with customer needs while maintaining the 'best practice' philosophy. All of which adds up to a difficult juggling act.

Ultimately benchmarking is *continuous learning*; the more it is practised, the more can then be applied next time. This makes it potentially very powerful. However, the benchmarking experience needs to be managed to ensure it is continually recycled to complement the development of the company. Sustainable continuous improvement can be achieved only if the *status quo* is constantly challenged and excellence standards reset. Therefore, a company's approach to benchmarking requires constant attention and updating to maintain both the internal and external pace of development.

Consequently, benchmarking must be coaxed if optimum benefit is to be derived. The style and level of management involvement will vary according to the phase. Recognising this at the outset ensures the appropriate groundwork whilst maintaining an overall perspective of the end goal.

For ease of explanation, the development of benchmarking is split into four distinct 'ages'. In reality these will overlap (See Fig 12.1) and often be confusingly intertwined. The main point is to recognise the trend and inject the appropriate management emphases to foster development. As with any initiative, management is required throughout with attributes having background support status during one phase and becoming predominant during others. Management expertise relies on knowing how to balance these to best effect.

Phase 1 - Puberty

This stage is characterised by

☐ Confusion about the difference between competitive analysis and benchmarking and when the former becomes the latter;

☐ A lack of commitment to the need for change and uncertainty about the efficacy of benchmarking to instigate it;

☐ A belief that despite all evidence to the contrary a quick fix will still be possible;

☐ A feeling of just wanting to 'check out how good/ bad we are';

☐ A lack of conviction that the company will have the stamina to sustain a longer term initiative;

☐ A lack of appreciation of the everyday consequences of adopting a benchmarking culture, eg openness and sharing;

☐ Fear that it may involve considerable effort and resource but not provide the right solution in the end; and

☐ Concern about the strategic consequences of a benchmarking exercise.

All of these can be overcome by firm, positive leadership at the appropriate level and informed management aware of the consequences and culture change brought about through benchmarking. The general rule is to keep all signals clear, concise and comprehensible.

Whether benchmarking starts at the initiative and in the domain of the quality manager, or at strategic corporate level, solutions for optimum management will be the same. Benchmarking will require:

High level of commitment. Before any actual benchmarking activity can begin, somebody (the quality/customer service manager) or a group of people (senior executive team) must be firmly committed to the need for change and to benchmarking as one of the cornerstones for instigating it. The more strategic benchmarking is, the greater will be the demand for resources over time. Hence, it requires commitment at a commensurate level.

Enthusiastic vision and realistic interpretation. Change is always threatening. The more widespread the degree of change, the slower and more fragile will be the progress. From the outset change will be more welcome if it is enthusiastically conveyed as something which is demonstrably for the better. The most realistic vision is one which everyone believes they can have a part in growing, rather than one that is planted on them. Benchmarking, with its focus on best practice which already exists, must always be conveyed as a realistic interpretation of the future.

Conviction and clarity of purpose. The mission and objectives must be *understood* by all employees before a critical mass of support for change can be expected. It must be equally clear how they will be achieved through benchmarking.

Everyday language. People cannot achieve unless they understand. There is always a temptation with new initiatives to language-up; one of the problems being that anyone 'in-the-know' soon forgets that some of the terms are specific and uses them as if they were common phrases. As a rule of thumb it is best to avoid short forms (6-Sigma, SPC, Quality Improvement Process (QIP), (PONC) as well as any phrase which needs explanation (customer service voids, sunsetting, deliverables, performance drivers, straw man models, and so on). If a common, everyday language is not installed from the outset, people throughout the organisation will make assumptions and interpretations based on their perceptions. These will not necessarily concur with the organisation goals or even colleagues' perceptions. Misunderstandings will occur sooner or later.

Working definition. The early days of benchmarking will be characterised by: random visits *to* other companies; random visits *from* other companies; and no efficient process for capturing or sharing information. A working definition of the term itself *in the context of what it means to the organisation* is needed to focus the activity. It is not necessarily the same for everyone. Merely adopting another company's definition is not the solution. Management must *think* what it means to their company. It must also be capable of enduring over a period of time. If it is not relevant in the context of the prevailing language and culture it will have no effect on people's activities and will be soon forgotten.

Co-ordination. As awareness of benchmarking grows there is a tendency for many small pockets of activity and experiments to spring up throughout the organisation with numerous individuals or groups going off on forays or gathering data. Whilst this is a sign that people feel personally empowered to improve their work situation - and is to be encouraged - the activity will be more effective if co-ordinated from the outset. It is not necessary to install intricate systems; it is preferable to select one or two approachable, creative people to act as catalysts and information channels. Their role is to know who is doing what and where, put people in touch with one another, stop individuals re-inventing the wheel and generally help avoid duplication.

Training. The earlier people can receive education in the benchmarking technique the better. The temptation is to detail a few employees to find out more about whether this technique could be helpful, give them no training other than directions to the nearest bookshop or library, and expect them to return in a relatively short space of time with usable data and cogent arguments! It is easier to install good habits from the start than to cure bad ones later. Hence, the emphasis should be on the overall approach and how it can help attain objectives. It is better to instil an early awareness of the need for diligence in applying the plan, analysis, action, review cycle than to focus too heavily on the individual steps.

Phase 2 - Youth

The most important management activity at this stage is drawing together all the threads and pointing the benchmarking activity in one direction. This includes putting in place the administrative mechanisms that will secure the long term efficacy of the programme.

In the early days of exploratory visits and internal benchmarking the more activity the better (provided it is useful, co-ordinated and informed) to grow critical mass for the technique. However, benchmarking almost always leads to change and this must be managed, directed and focused. The more decentralised the organisation, the greater the need for clear management, particularly if several business sectors are likely to prioritise similar processes for benchmarking at the same time.

The characteristics as this phase progresses are:

- [ ] Lack of priority;
- [ ] Confusing demands on resources;
- [ ] Growing conflict between desire for instant success and longer term improvements;
- [ ] Differing levels of awareness and commitment;
- [ ] Differing degrees of reaction to the technique ranging from resistance and rejection to acceptance and commitment;
- [ ] Number of different groups and interests involved;
- [ ] Conflict between personal and benchmarking objectives;
- [ ] Varying levels of training needs;
- [ ] Confusion over findings and their implication for operations or strategy;
- [ ] Uncertainty over degree of internal support, recognition and reward for activities; and
- [ ] Uncertainty about the level of external acceptance.

Particular emphasis on the following areas could 'solve' many of these uncertainties.

Leadership. Someone must lead the overall process. this is preferably a senior executive with the overview to ensure that the initiatives fit with the direction and purpose of the strategy, and that they are prioritised to the mission, goals and objectives. It will be the 'leader's' responsibility to avoid conflicts of interest. The leader will be accountable to the Board and the benchmark teams for trade-offs where necessary to make sure that the right things are done at the right time and in the best interests of the company.

Line-management commitment. Middle and line management are always in the 'firing-line'. At most they can handle effectively only one or two changes or new initiatives in any year. Each involves meetings, time for gaining acceptance, learning and installing new systems, procedures, documentation and so on. Meanwhile, this cannot detract from the day-to-day work which must continue undisturbed! One of the most effective ways of securing commitment and gaining support at this level is to integrate benchmarking into management plans and objectives. This then sets the expectations which should be reviewed in annual appraisals. Inclusions should encompass:

- Which processes require improvement and why;
- Which organisations are believed to employ better practice in those processes;
- How many should be investigated;
- Number of best practices found, where and how; and
- Improvement plans implemented as a result.

Training. General training in the technique should continue to penetrate through the organisation during this phase to ensure a consistent message and understanding. It is also necessary to introduce more specific emphases. In particular, there is greater need to concentrate on progressing individual steps to produce usable findings. Usually this will involve meshing benchmarking efforts and findings with other total quality initiatives so they are supportive of and complementary to one another.

The findings from the planning and analysis steps may not always correspond to expectations. The second need, therefore, is to ensure that the presentations of findings are well informed and prepared. These must be thoroughly understood and comparable with the *status quo* before being reported. They may, for example, need to be tailored to the audience's personal business agenda. A skilled presentation can often do more than facts and figures to influence the decision to support further efforts or accept recommendations.

Training must move forward and be up-dated as expertise develops. Ideally, it should incorporate learning from benchmarking team members and case studies from exercises carried out. This helps keep development at a practical level as well as standardising the technique, language and methodology used. Furthermore, it promotes consistency and team based learning.

Networks, facilitators, mentors. Throughout the second phase it will be increasingly desirable to establish foundations for informal networks which will evolve as benchmarking advances. Mini internal networks help to cross-fertilise views, ideas and perceptions reducing the opportunities for tunnel vision.

Identifying and developing facilitators and mentors will promulgate use of the technique and reduce delay or confusion as people try to sort out intermittent queries and problems. It may be necessary to refer to outside professional help until sufficient internal expertise is developed. In this case availability, and lines of communication, should be clearly 'advertised'.

Centre of excellence. A proven way of providing consistent back-up support is to formalise a centre of excellence. This will include the internal facilitator and/ or mentor. It may be one person or more. It can keep up-to-date on internal activity (including any historical evidence from benchmarking-type exercises), formal events such as conferences and seminars and gather information at an informal level. Moreover, it is preferably linked to external networks to provide a filter, as well as the centre, for benchmarking data and information.

The fundamental purpose is to relay relevant data and information (in and out) and provide the co-ordinated sorting and clearing house for all the company's benchmarking activity. As the link between internal and external networks, it is also the conduit for the two-way information sharing which is vital in an increasingly competitive environment.

Guidelines and protocol. With the best will in the world, it is not possible to train everybody on all new developments as they occur. Different levels of expertise and varying degrees of activity confuse those 'new' to the technique. It is beneficial to get the common message down in a user-friendly guide which is simple, consistent and easy to up-date.

The outward, sharing culture which develops with benchmarking can run counter to previous behaviour and provoke uncertainty or lack of confidence in people 'new' to dealing with the outside world. This may become particularly evident as the activity devolves more to operational levels. Developing guidelines on information sharing, general behaviour and presentation, the need for and nature of agreements, visit protocol and so on is beneficial without being bureaucratic. In fact, a clear guide can *prevent* the build-up of bureaucracy. It enables people to get on and improve their processes, within a reassuring and consistent framework, without the need for installing complicated checks and balances.

Phase 3 - Middle age

As activity moves increasingly towards concentration on external benchmarking the following characteristics predominate:

- ☐ Growing concern for the impact of findings on strategic planning;
- ☐ Corporate 'self-consciousness' arising from opening up to the outside world and letting others look in;
- ☐ Greater need for clarity of mission and purpose;
- ☐ Unwavering senior level commitment and support; and
- ☐ Increasing emphasis on establishing a common purpose and corporate 'pulling together'.

Emphasis on the following can help with these factors:

Integration with strategic change. At this stage it is vital that benchmarking is fully absorbed into the strategic planning process of the company. Whilst it may be feasible to sustain numerous internal benchmarking activities, constraints on resources and the need for the 'machine to keep on turning' make it unreasonable to focus on many external ones. By now, there is sufficient knowledge and expertise in the organisation to be able to concentrate on key critical success factors and aim for significant improvement over the long term.

The demand for consistency with strategy becomes more important as external activity develops because of the impact on the image and reputation of the company. If the objectives, mission and vision are sustainable and credible the company's image will more likely be strengthened than diminished. Equally, the clearer and more simple the terminology used the less likelihood of the meaning being distorted or misinterpreted by the outside world.

Maintain currency of information. It is important to find out what others are doing. Unfortunately, it is often the case that information, in journals or at conferences/seminars, is delivered with the benefit of hindsight. Thus the views given are retrospective. As time elapses the problems, barriers, enthusiasms, and lessons learned all diminish in people's minds. It is important to be aware of this and to find and create a dialogue or mini-network with companies *at the same stage of development*. If information is gathered solely from proven technicians or experts in the approach it can be difficult to assimilate and even have a demotivating effect.

In the European culture, there is a tendency for companies to remain reticent until progress and improvement can be verified. This should diminish as more organisations incorporate benchmarking into their activities. Meanwhile, obtaining current information remains a constant challenge!

Greater integration with personal objectives. The process of incorporating benchmarking goals into personal objectives should by now be cascading through the organisation to promote a common cause and purpose. The reward and remuneration policies should be amended gradually and weighted to reflect formal recognition for achievement. Certainly it will prove difficult to sustain enthusiasm and motivation for benchmarking if this does not happen.

Recognition. Benchmarking is invariably a team activity and there should be formal rewards for excellence in team effort and achievement, as well as for individuals and team leaders. Successes and improvements should be reported always but remember to keep the initiative 'real' internally by including some anecdotal and humorous news coverage. Over time, some successes will develop almost legendary status (as has become the case, for instance with L L Bean/Xerox Corporation). These can be developed to provide useful and provoking case studies for use in training.

Phase 4 - Maturity

Not many companies have been benchmarking long enough to reach this phase. However, the predominant characteristics appear to be:

- ☐ The need to sustain motivation and energy for the approach;
- ☐ Whilst also maintaining the humility to recognise that improvement is still possible and desirable; and
- ☐ Developing the flexibility to provide positive assistance to other organisations with least possible interruption or disruption to the business.

Predominant management features during this phase include:

Rejuvenate roles. In all probability strategic studies will continue over an extended period. Rotating the roles of team members and facilitators can help reduce the risk of people becoming desensitised to the approach. With certain key positions, such as team leaders, it may be preferable to rotate with another team rather than members of the same team. This will depend largely on the characteristics and strengths of individuals.

Keep it simple and fun! Just because an initiative has serious implications and consequences does not mean that all aspects must be conducted with strict and straight-faced dedication. Benchmarking will have far greater effect over the long term if fun, humour and light-heartedness are encouraged. One company runs a regular humorous poster competition. Staff are asked to submit an entry which encapsulates the essence of benchmarking. The winning entry, in addition to earning a significant personal prize for the 'author', then becomes the 'Message for the Month'. It is circulated in the company newsletter, on notice boards and any occasion where benchmarking is referred to.

Variations on this, or a similar theme can be applied in most organisations.

Grow inside-out. Good companies recognise they can improve continuously. However, maintaining humility and the will to see where improvement is possible is not always easy. Inviting objective outsiders into the organisation may provide a way through this. Regular, or even occasional, 'meeting' events with customers, suppliers and with recognised proponents of 'best practice' can present useful sharing and learning opportunities.

Best practice should not become a burden.
Growing a reputation for best practice in any process is sometimes seen as a blessing in disguise. There are many thousands of business processes; every company has different critical success factors and strategic plans. Consequently the number of companies benchmarking any given process, or likely to attain the accolade of 'best' at any single process will inevitably remain small.

In the maturity stage, therefore, the organisation needs to be clear about how it responds to requests from others to benchmark a renowned best practice. A policy should be drawn up clearly identifying how and why to deflect industrial voyeurism whilst developing suitable partnerships. This must be communicated efficiently so that everyone in the organisation can deal with requests and queries regarding benchmarking assistance.

BENCHMARKING MISSION

Nothing provides a better foundation for benchmarking than a clear, succinct mission statement coupled with an equally crisp explanation of how benchmarking will help in its achievement. The following example from Royal Mail UK is one of the best:

'Our mission is to be recognised as the best organisation in the world distributing text and packages.'

Benchmarking is: 'A structural process for learning from the practice of others, internally or externally, who are leaders in a field or with whom legitimate comparisons can be made.'

Quality Improvement Process: 'How can we do this better?'

Benchmarking: 'How can we do this better by learning how others do it?'

Famous last words

"Everything important that ever will be invented has already been invented."

(Attributed to the chief of the Prussian Patents Office, 1888.)

"Heavier than air flying machines are impossible."

(Lord Kelvin, president of the Royal Society, 1895.)

"Who the hell wants to hear actors talk?"

(Harry M Warner, Warner Brothers Pictures, 1927.)

"I see no future in these new-fangled machines."

(T Watson Snr about the computer in 1950.)

"There is no reason for any individual to have a computer in their home."

(Ken Olsen, president of Digital Equipment, 1977.)

Appendix A

Worksheets

SAMPLE WORKSHEETS 1-7 relate back to the text of the Planning Stage (Chapters Six and Seven). Worksheet 8 relates to the text of Chapter Nine in the Action Stage. They are intended as guides or prompts.

Page numbers indicating the relevant page of the text to which the Worksheets relate are indicated in brackets () at the bottom of each.

WORKSHEET ONE

IDENTIFYING THE SUBJECT AREA - 1*

1   WHAT BUSINESS IS YOUR COMPANY IN?

    ....

2   WRITE BELOW THREE FACTORS WHICH ARE CRITICAL TO YOUR COMPANY
    FOR SUCCESS IN THIS BUSINESS

    i ....

    ii ....

    iii ....

3   WHICH OF THESE HAS THE BIGGEST INFLUENCE ON YOUR COMPANY'S
    PERFORMANCE?

    ....

4   WHICH, IF IMPROVED, WOULD HAVE THE MOST SIGNIFICANT IMPACT ON
    CUSTOMER/EMPLOYEE/SUPPLIER RELATIONSHIPS?

    ....

5   WHICH, IF IMPROVED, WOULD CONTRIBUTE MOST TO BOTTOM LINE
    RESULTS?

    ....

6   WHICH IS OF GREATEST IMPORTANCE TO THE SUCCESSFUL CONTINUED
    DEVELOPMENT AND FUTURE OF THE BUSINESS?

    ....

(*See Chapter Six, page 68)

WORKSHEET TWO

IDENTIFYING THE SUBJECT AREA - 2*

TAKING YOUR RESPONSE TO QUESTION 6 ON WORKSHEET 1, NAME BELOW:-

1   THE MAJOR INPUTS

   i . . . .

   ii . . . .

   iii . . . .

   iv . . . .

   v . . . .

2   THE MAJOR OUTPUTS

   i . . . .

   ii . . . .

   iii . . . .

   iv . . . .

   v . . . .

(*See Chapter Six, page 68)

WORKSHEET THREE

THE BUSINESS SUPPLY CHAIN*

COMPLETE THE BOXES BELOW FOR YOUR BUSINESS/FUNCTION/JOB SUPPLY CHAIN. ADD FURTHER BOXES IF NECESSARY.

WORKSHEET FOUR

PEELING THE ONION*

1   NAME A PROCESS WITH WHICH YOU ARE DIRECTLY INVOLVED

. . . .

THIS IS REPRESENTED BY 'X' IN THE DIAGRAM BELOW:

2   CAN YOU NAME THE PROCESS AT 'B' OF WHICH IT IS A SUB-PROCESS?

. . . .

3   CAN YOU NAME THE PROCESS AT 'C' WHICH IS A SUB-PROCESS OF 'X'?

. . . .

4   CAN YOU ALSO NAME PROCESSES AT 'A', 'D' AND 'E'?

A . . . .

D . . . .

E . . . .

(*See Chapter Six, page 73)

WORKSHEET FIVE

PROCESS STEPS*

PROCESS NAME: . . . .

CHARTED BY: . . . .

DATE: . . . .

Details of method process steps	Type of activity	Measurement notes
1	. . . .	. . . .
2	. . . .	. . . .
3	. . . .	. . . .
4	. . . .	. . . .
5	. . . .	. . . .
6	. . . .	. . . .
7	. . . .	. . . .
8	. . . .	. . . .
9	. . . .	. . . .
10	. . . .	. . . .
11	. . . .	. . . .
12	. . . .	. . . .
13	. . . .	. . . .
14	. . . .	. . . .
15	. . . .	. . . .
16	. . . .	. . . .
17	. . . .	. . . .
18	. . . .	. . . .
19	. . . .	. . . .
20	. . . .	. . . .

(*See Chapter Six, page 80)

WORKSHEET SIX

SELECTING PARTNERS*

TAKING AS YOUR STARTING POINT ONE OF THE PROCESSES IDENTIFIED ON WORKSHEET 4:

NAME:

    a)   TWO POSSIBLE INTERNAL PARTNERS

    i) ....

    ii) ....

    b)   TWO POSSIBLE EXTERNAL PARTNERS

    i) ....

    ii) ....

    c)   TWO POSSIBLE BEST PRACTICE PARTNERS

    i) ....

    ii) ....

(*See Chapter Seven, page 94)

WORKSHEET SEVEN

DATA COLLECTION*

COMPLETE THE FORM BELOW FOR YOUR DATA COLLECTION

DATA SOURCE	RESPONSIBILITY ASSIGNED TO (NAME)	METHOD+	COLLECT BY (DATE)	CONFIRM COMPLETE
Internal:				
1.				
2.				
3.				
External:				
1.				
2.				
3.				

+Specify whether phone, fax, survey, visit, interview, observation etc.

(*See Chapter Seven, page 98)

WORKSHEET EIGHT

ACTION PLAN*

GOAL (a) ....

....

ACTION	BY WHOM	DEADLINE	COMPLETE
(b)			(c)
(List in step sequence)	(Name)	(dates/ milestones)	(yes/no) (if no why ?) (alternative course ?)
1. _____	1. _____	1. _____	
2. _____	2. _____	2. _____	
3. _____	3. _____	3. _____	

NOTES:

1. ACTION PLANS SHOW A DESIRED STATE (a) AT A FIXED POINT IN THE FUTURE, TOGETHER WITH REALISTIC STEPS (b) FOR ACHIEVING THIS

2. SOME ACTIONS AT (b) WILL BE PARALLEL, SOME WILL BE IN SERIES.

3. WHENEVER "NO" OCCURS AT (c) THOROUGH REVIEW IS ESSENTIAL PARTICULARLY WITH REGARD TO ITS IMPACT ON (a).

4. ENSURE ALTERNATIVE COURSES OF ACTION ACCURATELY COMMUNICATED.

(*See Chapter Nine, page 124)

Further reading

Books

Benchmarking: The search for industry best practices that lead to superior performance, by Robert C Camp, American Society for Quality Control (ASQC), published by Quality Press 1989 ISBN 0 87389 058 2

The road to quality, by D M Lascelles and B G Dale, IFS Publications, UK, 1993

Competitive benchmarking: An executive guide, by Dr Mohamed Zairi, Technical Communications (Publishing) Ltd, 1992 ISBN 0 946655 51 0

Booklets

Best practice benchmarking by the Department of Trade & Industry, prepared and published under the Enterprise Initiative Programme. Available from DTI marketing offices: (0443 821877 or Freephone 0800 500 700)

An introductory guide to benchmarking by ICI Chemicals & Polymers Ltd, available from Quality Library, ICI C&P (Tel: 021 377 6540; Fax: 021 377 6522)

Articles/Extracts/References

The evolution of benchmarking as a computer performance evaluation technique. *MIS Quarterly*, Mar 1985: Article by B C Lewis (Georgia State University) & A E Crews (Data General Corp).

Cutting costs without killing the business. *Fortune*, 13 Oct 1986: Article by Maggie McComas.

How to measure yourself against the best. *Harvard Business Review*, 1987 (v.87): Article by F G Tucker, S M Zivan, R C Camp.

Benchmarking: The key to developing competitive advantage in mature markets. *Planning Review*, Sep/Oct 1987: Article by Timothy R Furey (VP of Michael M Kaiser Assoc, Virginia, specialising in industry and competitive analysis and benchmarking).

How to benchmark logistics operations. *Distribution,* Aug 1988: Article by Dr J Cavinato.

Corporate spies snoop to conquer. *Fortune*, 7 Nov 1988: Article by Brian Dumaine.

Competing with tomorrow. *The Economist*, 12 May 1990. (Why keeping your eyes open is not enough. Ref to Gary Hamel, London Business School.)

Perspectives - Benchmarking. *Total Quality Management,* Dec 1990: Article by Paul Davies, Dir TQM International Ltd.

The benchmarking bandwagon. *Quality Progress*, Jan 1991: Article by Karen Bemowski.

AT&T's 12-step benchmarking process. *Quality Progress*, Jan 1991: Article by Karen Bemowski.

Benchmarking world-class performance. *The McKinsey Quarterly*, No 1 1991: Article by A S Walleck, J D O'Halloran and C A Leader.

Unleashing a plant revitalisation. *The McKinsey Quarterly*, No 1 1991: Article by D M Harlan Jr.

First find your bench. *The Economist,* 11 May 1991. (Refer to Benchmarking world class performance, by Steven Walleck, David O'Halloran and Charles Leader - *The McKinsey Quarterly* 1991 No 1.)

Collaborate with your competitors - and win*. *Harvard Busines Review*, Jan/Feb 1989: Article by Gary Hamel, Y L Doz and C K Prahalad. Reference to existing international collaborations.

Beyond products: Services-based strategy*, *Harvard Business Review*, Mar/Apr 1990: Article by J B Quinn, T L Doorley and P C Pacquette. (Focus on what gives your company its competitive edge. Outsource the rest. Competitive analysis should consider ... all potential providers and industries that might cross compete in the activity using 'best in the activity' as the relevant benchmark.)

The core competence of the corporation*. *The Harvard Business Review*, May/June 1991: Article by C K Prahalad and Gary Hamel.

Britain's most admired companies*. *The Economist,* 26 Jan 1991. (In association with Loughborough University's department of management studies, asks 1,800 of Britain's businessmen and financial analysts to name their corporate heroes.)

---

* Articles not specifically about benchmarking but elements of the technique included.

Useful contacts

The British Quality Foundation

Vigilant House, 120 Wilton Street, London SW1V 1JZ
Tel: +44 071 931 0607 Fax: +44 071 233 7034

The Centre for Interfirm Comparison

Capital House, 48 Andover Road, Winchester, Hampshire SO23 7BH
Tel: +44 0962 844144 Fax: +44 0962 843180

The Department of Trade & Industry

Kingsgate House, 67-74 Victoria Street, London SW1E 6SW
Tel: +44 071 215 7877 or Freefone 0800 500 200

The European Foundation for Quality Management

Avenue des Pleiades 19, B-1200 Brussels, Belgium
Tel: +32 2 775 3511 Fax: +32 2 775 3535

Useful contacts continued

Oak Business Developers
Long Gables, Templewood Lane, Farnham Common,
Bucks SL2 3HJ
Tel: +44 0753 646854 Fax: +44 0753 646854

**Profit Impact of Market Strategy (PIMS)
Associates Ltd**
7th Floor, Moor House, London Wall, London EC2Y 5ET
Tel: +44 071 628 1155 Fax: +44 071 628 2455

The Benchmarking Centre Ltd
c/o Dexion, Maylands Avenue, Hemel Hempstead, Herts
HP2 7EW
Tel: +44 0442 250040 Fax: +44 0442 245386

Index

One thing we can all

learn

from benchmarking

is that

we can always

learn

from benchmarking